# THE PUBLIC VAULTS UNLOCKED

# THE PUBLIC VAULTS UNLOCKED

## DISCOVERING AMERICAN HISTORY IN THE NATIONAL ARCHIVES

The Foundation for the National Archives, Washington, DC
in association with D Giles Limited, London

First published in 2005 by GILES
an imprint of D Giles Limited
57 Abingdon Road, London, W8 6AN, UK
*www.gilesltd.com*

ISBN (paperback): 0-9758601-1-9
ISBN (hardback): 1 904832 17 2

*The Public Vaults Unlocked: Discovering American History in the National Archives* is published to accompany The Public Vaults, a permanent exhibition at the National Archives Building in Washington, DC.

Library of Congress Control Number: 2005926147

Project Manager: Jane McAllister, Washington, DC
Copy editor: Maureen MacDonald, National Archives and Records Administration, Washington, DC
Designer: James Warner for Anikst Design, London *(www.anikstdesign.com)*

Produced by GILES, an imprint of D Giles Limited, London
Printed and bound in China

∞ The paper used in this publication meets the minimum requirements of the American National Standard for Information Sciences—Permanence of Paper for Printed Library Materials ANSI Z39.48-1984.

Cover: A variety of records from the National Archives (see captions pp. 57, 77, 91, 99, 153)
Back cover and endsheets: Stacks in the National Archives Building, Washington, DC
Frontispiece: Entrance to The Public Vaults exhibition
Pages 10–11: A video introduces The Public Vaults.

Photographic Credits
The majority of items reproduced in this book are from the holdings of the National Archives and Records Administration, which, unless otherwise noted, supplied the photographs. When applicable, identifying numbers, such as Still Picture Numbers for photographs held by the National Archives at College Park, Maryland, are included in the illustration captions. Installation photography is by Carol M. Highsmith (pp. 10–11, 12, 22–23, 89) and Brad Johnson (pp. 6, 14, 17). Stacks images (pp. 5, 21, 33, 41, 139, 170) and miscellaneous photos (pp. 9, 162–63, 168, 169) are by Earl McDonald, National Archives.

Page 108, Cuban President Fidel Castro in Havana, detail, 1963, © AP/Wide World Photos; page 118, Percy F. Allen, Assistant to the Chief Clerk and Chief of the Appointment Section, Department of State, using the Great Seal press, ca. 1924–39, courtesy of the U.S. Department of State; pages 171, 172–73, Photomosaic® by Robert Silvers, *www.photomosaic.com*. All rights reserved.

# CONTENTS

The "vaults" of the National Archives and Records Administration (NARA) have been "unlocked." Vast resources held by the National Archives in Washington, DC, and elsewhere can now be explored in a permanent exhibition, The Public Vaults, installed in the National Archives Building in Washington. Like the redesign of the Rotunda's treasured trio of America's founding documents—the Declaration of Independence, the Constitution, and the Bill of Rights—The Public Vaults is part of the multi-component National Archives Experience. And what an experience! Moving from the records of ordinary American families to films of modern Presidents as youngsters, from the papers documenting the evolution of American Government from its origins to those of post–Civil War African Americans assisted by the Freedmen's Bureau, visitors to The Public Vaults discover the nation's history anew. The mosaic of documentary set pieces and exciting interactive modules that make up The Public Vaults dramatically deepens the visitor's experience of the National Archives and the role it plays in American life.

Creative achievements such as The Public Vaults require the skills and collaboration of enormously talented individuals. A number of those responsible for this exhibit are acknowledged elsewhere in this book, but several deserve special mention. National Archives' Director of Museum Programs Marvin Pinkert provided leadership for the entire National Archives Experience project. He has been ably assisted by Christina Rudy Smith, Head of Exhibits for Museum Programs. The Executive Director of the Foundation for the National Archives, Thora Colot, and her staff offered the support and spearheaded the commitment needed to develop The Public Vaults program. Finally, without the efforts of my predecessor, the Eighth Archivist of the United States, John Carlin, and NARA's other senior officials, The Public Vaults could not have been initiated much less completed.

All those involved in the project deserve the gratitude of visitors who now pass through the building daily, delighting in and learning from the unlocking of the National Archives' documentary cornucopia. In short order, the National Archives has replaced the "behind the scenes" vaults previously unavailable to most Americans with our amazing Public Vaults.

Allen Weinstein
Ninth Archivist of the United States

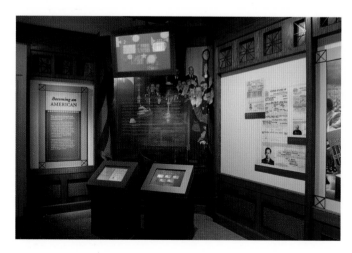

The *Becoming an American* unit in the "We the People" vault

This publication accompanies the highly immersive, permanent exhibition The Public Vaults, which highlights the historical records kept by the National Archives and Records Administration (NARA) of the United States of America. Featuring hundreds of original and facsimile records from NARA's nationwide holdings, as well as dynamic computer-aided and mechanical interactive exhibits, The Public Vaults is designed to simulate the experience of going behind the scenes at the National Archives into its vaults and stacks. Through the state-of-the-art exhibition and this accompanying publication, the National Archives is able to showcase its vast holdings, demonstrate the importance of Government records, and encourage visitors to use the National Archives, whether in Washington or at one of NARA's nationwide facilities. Our goal has been to convey the excitement of the National Archives' records, attract many audiences, stimulate, educate, and ultimately, we hope, inspire the public in thinking about how the nation's past can become a living instrument for directing the nation's future.

The primary contributors to this publication—Thora Colot, Marvin Pinkert, Christina Rudy Smith, Bruce I. Bustard, William Sandoval, and Stephanie Moore—are deeply grateful to all those who together brought The Public Vaults to life. Such an ambitious task could not have been achieved without the commitment and hard work of many people. Staff members of NARA's Museum Programs and those of NARA's important partner, the Foundation for the National Archives, spearheaded the highly collaborative effort, which depended on NARA staff in Washington, DC, and in regional facilities such as the Presidential libraries, as well as dedicated individuals from outside organizations. Archivists, conservators, registrars, librarians, research assistants, administrators, security personnel, educators, case makers, art handlers, graphic designers, audiovisual technicians, lighting and sound specialists, public affairs specialists, and more all played an important role in making The Public Vaults exhibition a success, and we regret that we cannot individually name each of them here. We are pleased, however, to be able to acknowledge those individuals who were directly involved in the making of this book.

On the Exhibits staff, Stacey Bredhoff, Senior Exhibits Curator, generously shared the research represented by her recent publications The Charters of Freedom: "A New World Is at Hand" (Washington, DC, and London: Foundation for the National Archives in association with D Giles, 2004) and American Originals (Washington, DC, Seattle, and London: National Archives and Records Administration in association with University of Washington Press, 2001). From the latter publication in particular, we borrowed text for some entries. We have also excerpted portions of text from our own writings and from writings by Ellen Fried of the editorial staff of NARA's quarterly journal, Prologue, that have appeared in that publication. Exhibits Support Specialist Darlene McClurkin helpfully carried out much of the media research for the exhibition and publication, and Maureen MacDonald copyedited the text for the same. James Zeender, Registrar for Exhibits, coordinated the 237 images that are reproduced in this publication, and Steve Puglia, Jeffrey Reed, and Erin Rhodes were responsible for scanning documents, downloading digital files for the publisher's use, and approving the color proofs. Conservators Catherine Nicholson and Mary Lynn Ritzenthaler reviewed sections of the publication relating to the preservation of the Charters of Freedom. In addition to NARA's own photographers, especially Earl McDonald and Amy Young, we wish to thank Carol Highsmith and Brad Johnson for the additional installation photography; the U.S. Department of State for the photograph of Percy F. Allen using the Great Seal press (p. 118); and Robert Silvers for permission to use the Photomosaic® (pp. 171, 172–73). Thanks also go to Mary Finch, George Bush Library, and Maryrose Grossman, John F. Kennedy Library.

The staff of the Foundation for the National Archives, led by Executive Director Thora Colot, was instrumental in making the exhibit and publication a reality. We want to thank Franck Cordes, Executive Administrator, and especially Christina Gehring, Special Projects Assistant, who managed this project for the Foundation and assisted with various details associated with this publication.

Daniel Giles, Managing Director of D Giles Limited, London, enthusiastically took on this project, the second volume the Foundation for the National Archives has published in association with D Giles. We are grateful to Dan for bringing freelance editor Jane McAllister on board as Project Manager in Washington, DC; Jane worked closely with the contributors to cull texts and images from the exhibition and reshape them for publication. In London, Sarah McLaughlin, Production Director for D Giles, kept track of the many digital files and oversaw all production aspects. For Anikst Design, James Warner has produced a handsome design that skillfully integrates many components.

Eighth Archivist John W. Carlin led the National Archives in charting new directions. The Public Vaults exhibition and publication provide extraordinary opportunities to teach the public about the National Archives in ways that were never before possible. We are honored to be a part of this significant, ongoing enterprise.

T.C., M.P., C.R.S., B.I.B., W.S., and S.M.

## The Contributors

Thora Colot, Executive Director of the Foundation for the National Archives, with twenty-eight years of museum experience, was appointed in 2002 by the Foundation's Board of Directors to oversee all the Foundation's operations. She has a B.A. in Theater Design and Studio Arts from the University of Virginia and an M.A. in Museum Studies from George Washington University.

Marvin Pinkert, Director of Museum Programs, joined the National Archives in 2000 to lead the project to create the National Archives Experience, after eleven years at the Museum of Science and Industry in Chicago. He holds a Master of Management from the J.L. Kellogg School of Management at Northwestern University, an M.A. in Japanese studies from Yale University, and a B.A. in English from Brandeis University.

Christina Rudy Smith, Head of Exhibits, Museum Programs, began working for the National Archives in 1974, joining the Exhibits staff as a curator in 1976 and becoming head in 1983, and serving as curator for four major exhibits. Chris has a B.A. in Literature from American University and an M.A. in English from Stanford University.

Bruce I. Bustard, Senior Curator, Museum Programs, was the curator of "Picturing the Century: One Hundred Years of Photographs from the National Archives." He received his Ph.D. in History from the University of Iowa.

William Sandoval, Curator, Museum Programs, is a major in the Army Reserve. He has degrees in History from The Citadel and Monmouth University and a C.M.S. from Harvard University.

Stephanie Moore, Research Assistant, received a B.A. from the University of Maryland in 2003. She began working on The Public Vaults exhibit as a student intern in 2002.

For more than six decades, visitors have come to the National Archives to see the Declaration of Independence, the Constitution, and the Bill of Rights. Most have left without knowing that the National Archives holds millions more Federal records in trust for the American people—records that allow citizens to claim their rights, hold their government accountable, and learn about who we are as a nation and a people.

Realizing we needed to do a better job explaining the role records play in our lives, our nation, and our society, we designed a new project, the National Archives Experience, to reach out to the public. The Public Vaults, a major component of this project, is a new permanent exhibit that reveals how records are a vital link between America's past and its future.

The Public Vaults takes you on a virtual journey beyond the walls of the National Archives, deep into the stacks and files. Here you see the essential evidence of the story of America, which began with the founding documents and is still being written today. Interactive tools allow you to explore treaties, patent applications, acts of Congress, and Supreme Court decisions that changed the course of history. You also can find documents that tell your family's story, such as census schedules, immigration records, and homestead applications.

The Public Vaults and other components of the National Archives Experience were made possible through the support of the Foundation for the National Archives, a nonprofit group dedicated to bringing the nation's records to the public in exciting new ways. I would like to give special thanks to Willard Hackerman, Alan Voorhees, and Dell, Inc. for their generous support of The Public Vaults.

The Public Vaults is a place of discovery, through which, I hope, everyone gains an understanding of his or her personal connection to the records in the National Archives. I hope that families see how their stories fit into the national mosaic and that young people are thrilled by the real-life drama of the American experience. And I hope that individuals of all ages take action and use the National Archives— to learn, to unravel, to discover, and to celebrate the stories of individuals, families, communities, and the nation.

John W. Carlin
Eighth Archivist of the United States

A young visitor uses a computer interactive in the *Investigations* unit of the "Form a More Perfect Union" vault.

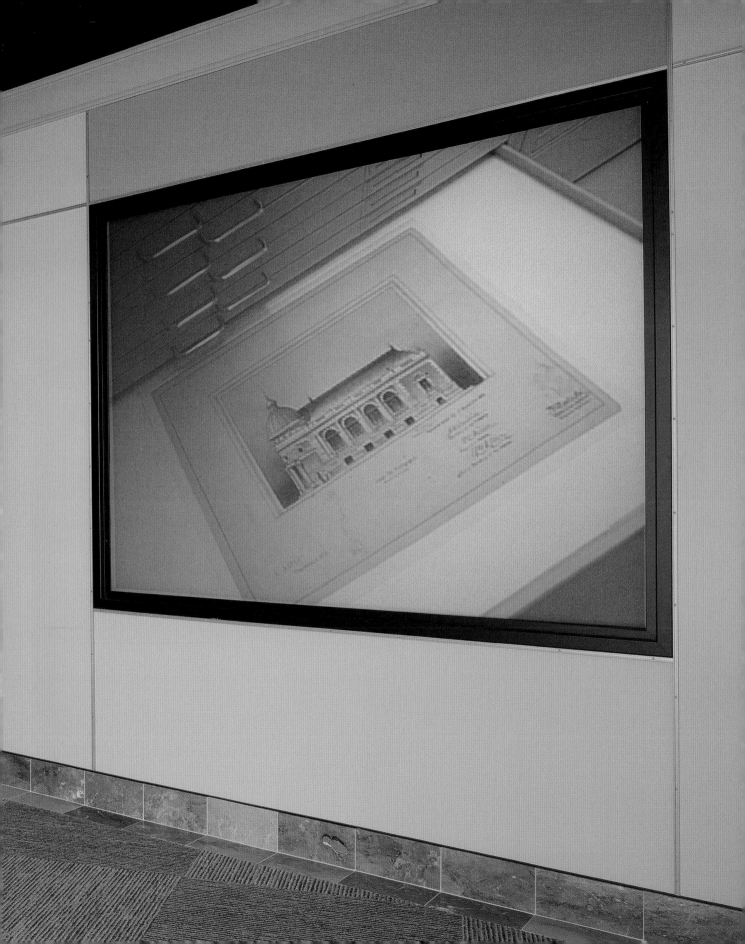

The National Archives and Records Administration (NARA) exists to preserve the permanently valuable records of the three branches of the United States Government and those that are essential to the lives of its citizens. Located on the National Mall in Washington, DC, halfway between the Capitol and the White House, the National Archives Building is literally at the center of Government. In addition, the National Archives encompasses other facilities in the Washington metropolitan area, such as its major research center at College Park, Maryland, as well as the nation's Presidential libraries and regional archives and records centers across the country.

The Charters of Freedom—the Declaration of Independence, the Constitution of the United States, and the Bill of Rights—are the most famous records housed by the National Archives, but they are just the tip of a vast iceberg. In its care are more than two centuries of Government records that preserve, legitimize, and perpetuate democracy in the United States. These millions of letters, memos, maps, drawings, photographs, films, and digital files are extraordinary. They include such priceless historical materials as the records of the Continental Congress; the Emancipation Proclamation; Mathew Brady's Civil War glass-plate negatives; the Warren Commission evidence; treaties with foreign governments; every national census since 1790; firsthand reports from the Battles of Lexington, Gettysburg, Midway, and Khe Sanh; and passenger manifests from Ellis Island. The records in the National Archives form a tangible legacy from the generations who built the United States.

The Public Vaults, installed in November 2004 as a permanent exhibition, presents, for the first time, the depth, diversity, and magnitude of the Federal Government's records. Never before have so many records from all of NARA's locations been on exhibit at once, brought to life through technology that accommodates more records than is possible to present through traditional exhibition or

**Entrance to the "We the People" vault**

**Chun Jan Yut with father, Chun Duck Chin, ca. 1899**

*National Archives–Pacific Region (San Bruno), Records of the Immigration and Naturalization Service*

publication formats. About 1,100 originals and facsimiles of documents, photographs, maps, drawings, and film or audio clips are featured in interactive tools that allow visitors to explore them in detail in innovative ways. Video loops showing large numbers of photographs, original sound recordings, motion pictures, computer-driven and mechanical devices, and graphic components, all presented in diverse and creative installations, create access and convey the experience of being behind the scenes at the National Archives. With this exhibition, the National Archives invites the public to go beyond the building's Rotunda, where the Charters of Freedom are displayed, to explore the raw materials of history—the rich and varied records that document great national events and the lives of individual Americans.

## Records Matter

More than a holding place for the Charters of Freedom and other records, the National Archives is an essential resource for American democracy, a place to discover why ongoing preservation, protection, and accessibility of records are crucial to safeguarding democratic freedoms. For more than six decades, the National Archives has been charged with those responsibilities for the American people. Yet millions of Americans do not know that the National Archives exists or that it holds Government records in trust for their use.

Records ensure continued access to essential evidence that document the rights and entitlements of American citizens. They make it possible to hold public officials and the actions of Government accountable. They tell the stories of common and extraordinary citizens and the larger story of the American experience. Some records mark individual journeys, while others mark the journey of the nation; all are the foundation of American democracy.

Records allow the American people to claim individual rights, to hold their government accountable, and to understand the nation's history. The work of the National Archives is a public trust that enables people to inspect for themselves the record of what Government has done. It enables officials and agencies to review their actions. And every day, every week, new records with new stories come to the National Archives so they can be made available for the public's use.

## More than Paper

When people think about Government records, what probably first comes to mind are written documents such as letters, memos, and forms, but the National Archives is a cultural institution with vast resources. In addition to the billions of paper records in its custody, the National Archives holds 41 million photographs; 300,000 reels of film; maps and charts; audio recordings; and 120,000 digital records.

Many of the most exciting items in The Public Vaults prove that the National Archives holds more than paper. A stroll through "Record of America," the central pathway that connects the rooms of The Public Vaults, traces the evolution of the technology by which information has been recorded;

Illustrated family record from
file of Joseph Smead,
Massachusetts, ca. 1845
*National Archives, Records of
the Veterans Administration*

opposite page:
*The Digital Challenge* unit in
the "To Ourselves and Our
Posterity" vault

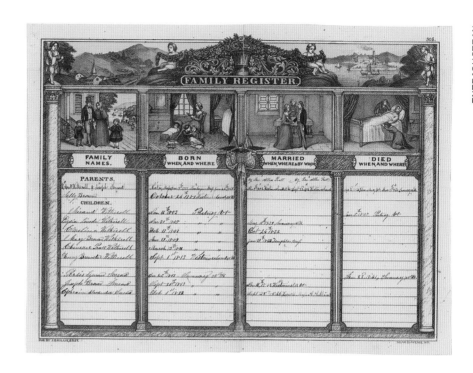

records here extend from one of George Washington's hand-written letters to the first Presidential web site. In between are a photograph from the Civil War; film clips of Theodore Roosevelt; a recording of one of Franklin Roosevelt's "fireside chat" radio broadcasts; a satellite image of Moscow; and an electronic database of Vietnam POWs.

Throughout the exhibition, sound recordings, film, posters, and electronic records are integrated with one another and with textual material to express the power of records. Recruiting films are paired with posters urging citizens to join the armed forces; immigration documents are used to create a guessing game; headphones transmit the voices of past Presidents; and television sets broadcast modern Presidential speeches. Through a variety of means, visitors are given the opportunity to experience and learn in the ways they like best—whether it's reading original handwritten documents; using touch-screen computers to

enlarge or highlight selected parts of a document, move them around, and read transcriptions of handwriting, all of which allow an individual to follow a thread of interest in a particular subject matter; manipulating a hands-on mechanical interactive; or listening, looking, and responding to the audiovisuals, which for many provide great emotional appeal.

## We're All Here

"Federal records" conjures up images of the monumental documents that shaped the United States: Constitutional amendments, acts of Congress, Presidential proclamations, and court decisions. While it is true that these documents all have a place in the National Archives, many "treasures" are far more personal. Such records touch on the lives of ordinary citizens—people trying to make a new home, a new community, and sometimes a new life; people exer-

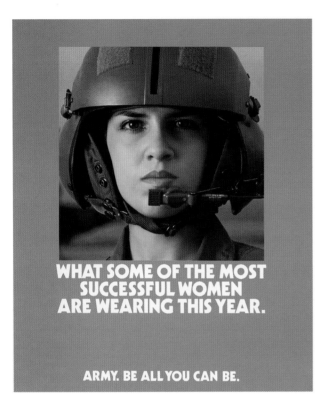

"What Some of the Most Successful Women Are Wearing This Year," U.S. Army recruiting poster, ca. 1990
*National Archives, Records of the United States Army Training and Doctrine Command (553-RP-Female-90-5)*

opposite page:
The *Presidents: Conflicts, Crises, and Peace* unit in "We the People"

cising their right to speak out; and people working and fighting for their country.

For many first-time visitors to the National Archives, The Public Vaults introduces the idea that their family's records and those of their friends and neighbors are housed together in the same facilities that hold the nation's great laws and historic speeches. While records such as immigration and naturalization papers, census schedules, draft registration cards, and homestead applications may lack the glamour created by the seals and stamps found on treaties and laws, these humble instruments of citizenship often contain some of the most interesting insights into people who are not usually considered part of the Government record.

Family records are most prominently displayed in the "We the People" vault. Exhibited in this section are dozens of family photos that came to the National Archives because they were part of a court case, an immigration file, or a Government photography project. Here, too, are the records of the Freedmen's Bureau, a post–Civil War agency that provided relief, established schools, and legalized marriages for former slaves to help them become self-sufficient. The interactive unit *Are You in the Archives?* lets visitors discover the many ways in which their relatives' records may have become part of the National Archives. In this unit a wall of movable panels poses such questions as "My great-aunt became a U.S. citizen in 1940. Is she in the Archives?" and then supplies answers. Original illustrated family records submitted by Revolutionary War veterans and their families to support pension claims showcase the family trees in the National Archives.

## Something for Everyone

The National Archives is for everyone. Visitors of every age and background are bound to find something in The Public Vaults that particularly engages them. People interested in the American Presidency, for example, will want to explore *First Families Growing Up* to guess which President or First Lady is pictured in childhood photos on display, or in *White*

*House: Inside Story* listen to excerpts from audiotapes made in the Oval Office by Presidents Roosevelt, Eisenhower, Kennedy, Johnson, and Nixon. *White House: Public Platform* presents film clips of Presidents as they respond to what President Coolidge complained was the "perpetual clamor for public utterances"; *Presidents: Conflicts, Crises, and Peace* looks at critical foreign policy and military decisions and allows visitors to eavesdrop as John Kennedy discusses Soviet missiles in Cuba and Dwight Eisenhower grapples with a crisis in the Suez.

While this publication illustrates only a small portion of the images visitors see in the exhibition, and it cannot reproduce all that visitors experience there, it does present activities that ask readers to participate actively. In the *Patent Puzzlers* game (pp. 154–55), for example, children can examine drawings and try to match them to the patent inventions they illustrate. The *Signed and Sealed* unit explores the symbolism of the Great Seal, then asks readers to design their own versions (p. 119). In these and other activities, readers will test their knowledge and be creative.

Military history buffs visiting the exhibition have the opportunity to do what thousands of filmmakers have done at the National Archives: use silent footage taken during the Allied invasion to create a short film about D-day. The exhibition also lets visitors compare the 1989 film *Glory*, about the 54th Massachusetts Infantry Regiment, an African American army unit during the Civil War, with the records of the regiment held by the National Archives.

All the exhibits in The Public Vaults point out the astonishing breadth and diversity of the National Archives' holdings and offer myriad opportunities to find something fascinating. There is something here for everyone.

Like the exhibition, this publication is designed to guide the public to discover personal stories in the fabric of America's history. The book's six illustrated chapters follow the organization of the exhibition. "Record of America" offers a "fast track," or overview, of the exhibition and indeed of the holdings of the National Archives, through original documents that span time and technology. The other five chapters are based on the thematically based "vaults" of the exhibition, which take their titles from the Preamble to the Constitution.

In "Record of America" the focus is not on milestone documents written by famous individuals but on the transformation of records that tell the nation's story. Representing the various media in the holdings of the National Archives, these items offer a journey not based on chronology, but rather, on changes in technology and record types. In these transformations are the clues to understanding our past. Here, original documents bring history alive by evoking—through images and stories—the immediacy of events captured in records of diverse media, whether an eighteenth-century treaty or broadside, a nineteenth-century telegram or photograph, or a twentieth-century satellite image or documentary film. Showcasing the evolution of media, the texts and images invite the reader to share American moments seen in different times and places through its records.

"We the People," which focuses on family and citizenship, provides a sense of who Americans are as a people. Readers will learn that the National Archives has records about not only important and famous people but also ordinary Americans. This vault of the exhibition shows how someone can establish U.S. citizenship, or how to research family history through documents such as immigration records, naturalization papers, census schedules, draft cards, and homestead applications. Visitors will also explore records about Native Americans, early settlers from Europe, people who instantly became Americans

when their region was annexed, and the story of freed slaves during Reconstruction.

In a democracy, records belong to the people. Whether you are a Government official or a private citizen, the National Archives encourages you to understand the role of records in your life. "Form a More Perfect Union" highlights records of liberty and law that illustrate the evolution of democracy in the United States. This section also looks at the ways lawyers, Government officials, and private citizens use records to maintain their rights. In this vault, visitors to the exhibition can hear congressional debates on Prohibition from 1918 and reinstating the draft from 1940 (and then vote). They can also investigate the materials and evidence preserved from twelve famous investigations, four of which—the Lincoln and Kennedy assassinations, Project

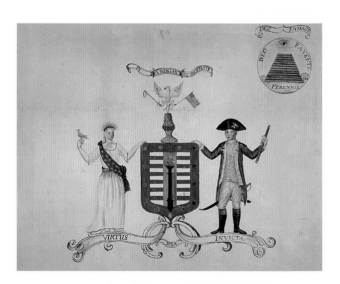

**William Barton's design for the Great Seal, May 1782**
*National Archives, Records of the Continental and Confederation Congresses and the Constitutional Convention*

opposite page:
**Patent drawing for "Velocipede," by C. E. Dayton, October 26, 1869**
*National Archives, Records of the Patent and Trademark Office*

Blue Book, the Nuremberg Trials, and Watergate—are discussed in this publication.

"Provide for the Common Defense" is about war and diplomacy. Records from the Revolutionary War through the Persian Gulf War paint a vivid picture of heroism, inspiration, and sacrifice. This section shows how the National Archives has preserved the records of those who have served in the military or as diplomats. It also demonstrates how historians and filmmakers use information found in the National Archives. Visitors to the unit *Presidents: Conflicts, Crises, and Peace* can listen to parts of actual conversations that took place in the White House; through these audiotapes, they learn how Presidents have made decisions in times of crises and the efforts they have taken to achieve peace.

Records in "Promote the General Welfare" celebrate the imagination and enterprise of Americans. Perhaps having special appeal to those who are interested in technology, this section emphasizes records of firsts and frontiers and shows how ingenuity and the human spirit have helped the nation realize the promise of America as envisioned by the Founders. The unit *July 20, 1969* transports visitors back to the day a person first landed on the Moon. *Patent Puzzlers* presents original patent drawings for a range of inventions that have changed our lives.

"To Ourselves and Our Posterity" focuses on the care and preservation of the National Archives' holdings—from early rare parchments to the latest electronic files—and the challenges that NARA and society face in preserving them. Readers and visitors to the exhibition will learn about the National Archives' role in keeping records for future generations, how a Government document becomes a record at NARA, and even how to care for family records. NARA is all across America, and the unit *NARA across America* presents a sampling from the seventeen regional records services facilities, the Presidential libraries, and the National Personnel Records Center in St. Louis. Research at the National Archives does not have to

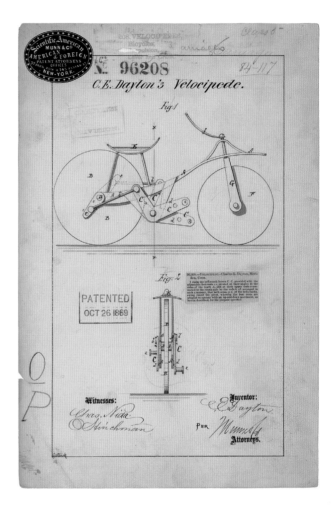

take place in Washington but can be accomplished in many cities and towns all over America. In addition, resources can be found online at *www.archives.gov*. As America grows and changes every day, so do its records. The chapters that follow illustrate how and why records matter—to individuals, families, and the nation.

**The Declaration of Independence printed from the 1823 copper plate engraved by William J. Stone, to commemorate the American Revolution Bicentennial, 1976**
*National Archives*

opposite page:
**Engraved copper printing plate, William J. Stone, 1823**
*National Archives, General Records of the Department of State*

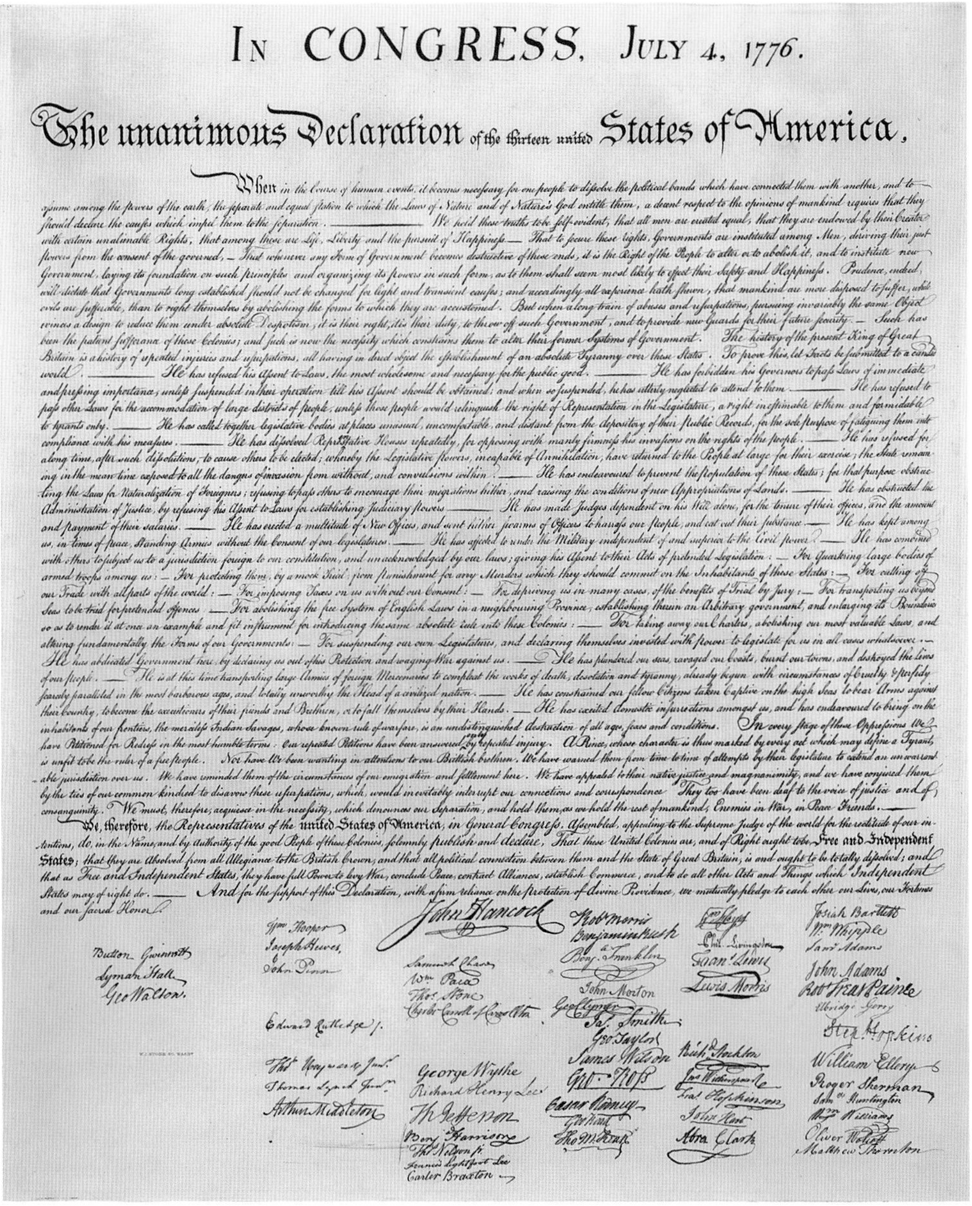

IN CONGRESS, JULY 4, 1776.

The unanimous Declaration of the thirteen united States of America,

When in the Course of human events, it becomes necessary for one people to dissolve the political bands which have connected them with another, and to assume among the powers of the earth, the separate and equal station to which the Laws of Nature and of Nature's God entitle them, a decent respect to the opinions of mankind requires that they should declare the causes which impel them to the separation. —— We hold these truths to be self-evident, that all men are created equal, that they are endowed by their Creator with certain unalienable Rights, that among these are Life, Liberty and the pursuit of Happiness. — That to secure these rights, Governments are instituted among Men, deriving their just powers from the consent of the governed, — That whenever any Form of Government becomes destructive of these ends, it is the Right of the People to alter or to abolish it, and to institute new Government, laying its foundation on such principles and organizing its powers in such form, as to them shall seem most likely to effect their Safety and Happiness. Prudence, indeed, will dictate that Governments long established should not be changed for light and transient causes; and accordingly all experience hath shewn, that mankind are more disposed to suffer, while evils are sufferable, than to right themselves by abolishing the forms to which they are accustomed. But when a long train of abuses and usurpations, pursuing invariably the same Object evinces a design to reduce them under absolute Despotism, it is their right, it is their duty, to throw off such Government, and to provide new Guards for their future security. — Such has been the patient sufferance of these Colonies; and such is now the necessity which constrains them to alter their former Systems of Government. The history of the present King of Great Britain is a history of repeated injuries and usurpations, all having in direct object the establishment of an absolute Tyranny over these States. To prove this, let Facts be submitted to a candid world. —— He has refused his Assent to Laws, the most wholesome and necessary for the public good. —— He has forbidden his Governors to pass Laws of immediate and pressing importance, unless suspended in their operation till his Assent should be obtained; and when so suspended, he has utterly neglected to attend to them. —— He has refused to pass other Laws for the accommodation of large districts of people, unless those people would relinquish the right of Representation in the Legislature, a right inestimable to them and formidable to tyrants only. —— He has called together legislative bodies at places unusual, uncomfortable, and distant from the depository of their Public Records, for the sole purpose of fatiguing them into compliance with his measures. —— He has dissolved Representative Houses repeatedly, for opposing with manly firmness his invasions on the rights of the people. —— He has refused for a long time, after such dissolutions, to cause others to be elected; whereby the Legislative powers, incapable of Annihilation, have returned to the People at large for their exercise; the State remaining in the mean time exposed to all the dangers of invasion from without, and convulsions within. —— He has endeavoured to prevent the population of these States; for that purpose obstructing the Laws for Naturalization of Foreigners; refusing to pass others to encourage their migrations hither, and raising the conditions of new Appropriations of Lands. —— He has obstructed the Administration of Justice, by refusing his Assent to Laws for establishing Judiciary powers. —— He has made Judges dependent on his Will alone, for the tenure of their offices, and the amount and payment of their salaries. —— He has erected a multitude of New Offices, and sent hither swarms of Officers to harrass our people, and eat out their substance. —— He has kept among us, in times of peace, Standing Armies without the Consent of our legislatures. —— He has affected to render the Military independent of and superior to the Civil power. —— He has combined with others to subject us to a jurisdiction foreign to our constitution, and unacknowledged by our laws; giving his Assent to their Acts of pretended Legislation: — For Quartering large bodies of armed troops among us: — For protecting them, by a mock Trial, from punishment for any Murders which they should commit on the Inhabitants of these States: — For cutting off our Trade with all parts of the world: — For imposing Taxes on us without our Consent: — For depriving us in many cases, of the benefits of Trial by Jury: — For transporting us beyond Seas to be tried for pretended offences — For abolishing the free System of English Laws in a neighbouring Province, establishing therein an Arbitrary government, and enlarging its Boundaries so as to render it at once an example and fit instrument for introducing the same absolute rule into these Colonies: — For taking away our Charters, abolishing our most valuable Laws, and altering fundamentally the Forms of our Governments: — For suspending our own Legislatures, and declaring themselves invested with power to legislate for us in all cases whatsoever. — He has abdicated Government here, by declaring us out of his Protection and waging War against us. —— He has plundered our seas, ravaged our Coasts, burnt our towns, and destroyed the lives of our people. —— He is at this time transporting large Armies of foreign Mercenaries to compleat the works of death, desolation and tyranny, already begun with circumstances of Cruelty & perfidy scarcely paralleled in the most barbarous ages, and totally unworthy the Head of a civilized nation. —— He has constrained our fellow Citizens taken Captive on the high Seas to bear Arms against their Country, to become the executioners of their friends and Brethren, or to fall themselves by their Hands. —— He has excited domestic insurrections amongst us, and has endeavoured to bring on the inhabitants of our frontiers, the merciless Indian Savages, whose known rule of warfare, is an undistinguished destruction of all ages, sexes and conditions. In every stage of these Oppressions We have Petitioned for Redress in the most humble terms: Our repeated Petitions have been answered only by repeated injury. A Prince, whose character is thus marked by every act which may define a Tyrant, is unfit to be the ruler of a free people. Nor have We been wanting in attentions to our Brittish brethren. We have warned them from time to time of attempts by their legislature to extend an unwarrantable jurisdiction over us. We have reminded them of the circumstances of our emigration and settlement here. We have appealed to their native justice and magnanimity, and we have conjured them by the ties of our common kindred to disavow these usurpations, which, would inevitably interrupt our connections and correspondence. They too have been deaf to the voice of justice and of consanguinity. We must, therefore, acquiesce in the necessity, which denounces our Separation, and hold them, as we hold the rest of mankind, Enemies in War, in Peace Friends. ——

We, therefore, the Representatives of the united States of America, in General Congress, Assembled, appealing to the Supreme Judge of the world for the rectitude of our intentions, do, in the Name, and by Authority of the good People of these Colonies, solemnly publish and declare, That these United Colonies are, and of Right ought to be Free and Independent States; that they are Absolved from all Allegiance to the British Crown, and that all political connection between them and the State of Great Britain, is and ought to be totally dissolved; and that as Free and Independent States, they have full Power to levy War, conclude Peace, contract Alliances, establish Commerce, and to do all other Acts and Things which Independent States may of right do. —— And for the support of this Declaration, with a firm reliance on the protection of divine Providence, we mutually pledge to each other our Lives, our Fortunes and our sacred Honor.

## Stone's Copper Plate

The Declaration of Independence is on display in the Rotunda of the National Archives Building.

What did the Declaration of Independence look like in 1776? As early as 1817 the Declaration of Independence had faded and become difficult to read. In 1820, Secretary of State John Quincy Adams asked William J. Stone, a Washington, DC, printer and engraver, to make a copper engraving that would reproduce the size, text, lettering, and signatures of the original. After finishing his printing plate in 1823, Stone printed 201 copies on parchment for Federal, state, and local officials, as well as for the descendants of the original signers. Today, only 31 of these original copies are known to exist. In 1976, printers from the U.S. Bureau of Engraving and Printing struck seven additional prints from Stone's copper plate to commemorate the Bicentennial of the American Revolution.

Stone's engraving shows us what the Declaration looked like when it was first written by hand. His printing plate is preserved within the records of the Department of State in the National Archives. Together, the print and copper plate offer a bridge between the original treasure in the Rotunda and the many vital records presented in The Public Vaults.

# RECORD OF AMERICA
## A JOURNEY THROUGH TIME AND TECHNOLOGY

Records matter—to us, to our future, to the future of our democracy. Records mark our passage through time, revealing where we came from and where we're going. As a sampler of the types of records found in the National Archives, the records in this section take you on a journey through time and technology, from an early Continental Congress broadside, to homestead forms and patent drawings, through contemporary satellite images and the first Presidential web site.

**The 1845 Treaty with Belgium on display in the "Record of America" hallway**

ENTER>

During the eighteenth century, letters were the primary means of communication, whether for personal messages among ordinary people or important news transmitted by the nation's leaders. As commander of the American armies during the Revolutionary War and later the nation's first President, George Washington observed the etiquette of the day and tried to answer every letter he received. Washington wrote many letters himself but also relied on the services of secretaries to keep up with the volume, which included the hundreds of letters written to Congress and other Government officials. The National Archives holds many of Washington's letters.

**Letter to the President of the Continental Congress congratulating Congress on the completion of the Confederation, March 21, 1781**
*National Archives, Records of the Continental and Confederation Congresses and the Constitutional Convention*

Although the text is in the handwriting of an aide, this letter is signed by George Washington. Here General Washington congratulates the President of Congress when, after nearly five years of struggling to create a "Confederation of the United States," Congress finally ratified the Articles of Confederation on March 1, 1781.

Today we can hear breaking news from around the globe twenty-four hours a day, but to Americans wanting urgent news about the Revolutionary War, the wait was often considerably longer. During the eighteenth century the most rapid form for circulating news was the broadside, a simple flyer printed on one side of a sheet of paper. Copies were posted in public places such as town halls and coffeehouses, read aloud in churches and public meetings, and often reprinted in local newspapers. The Revolutionary War Continental Congress relied on the broadside as the fastest means for disseminating important updates on the progress of the war and urging the American public to support the cause of independence.

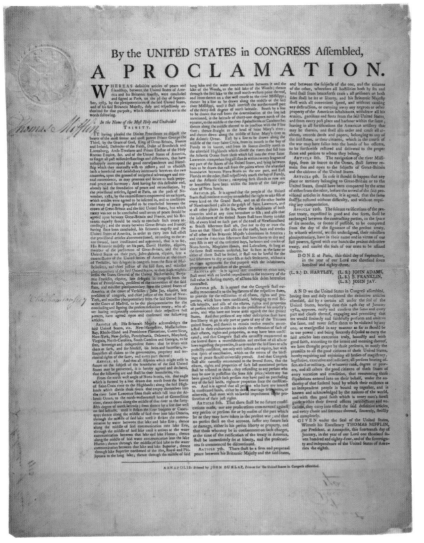

**Broadside announcing the Treaty of Paris, January 18, 1784**
*National Archives, Records of the Continental and Confederation Congresses and the Constitutional Convention*

On January 14, 1784, Congress ratified the Treaty of Paris, which John Adams, Benjamin Franklin, and John Jay had signed in Paris in September 1783. The ratification officially ended the Revolutionary War. This broadside, printed in Annapolis four days after the signing of the ratification, informed the public that the war was over. The broadside and the Treaty of Paris itself are among the earliest records in the National Archives.

Beginning in its founding session in 1789, Congress has passed tens of thousands of laws. Among the acts passed in the first session were appropriations, a tariff bill, and bills setting pay for Federal employees. The first session also established a number of this country's basic institutions—including the War, Treasury, and Foreign Affairs Departments.

The process of lawmaking has changed little since the First Congress, but the method of recording laws has been greatly transformed. Once handwritten on parchment, the text of laws are now keyed into a computer and produced on a laser printer. The final, or enrolled, copy of every act of Congress resides at the National Archives.

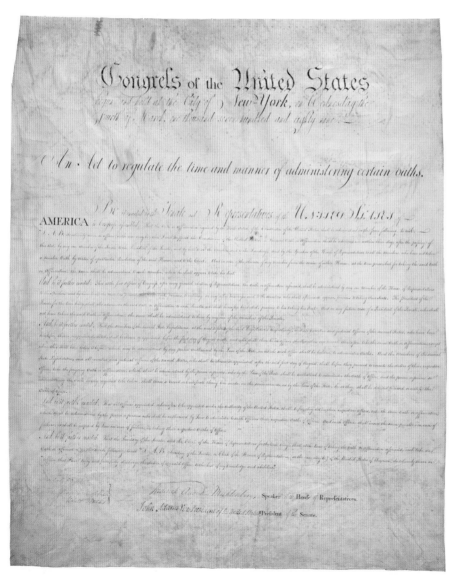

**The first act of Congress, June 1, 1789**
*National Archives, General Records of the U.S. Government*

On June 1, 1789, the First Congress passed the nation's first law. The law required all members of Federal, state, and local governments to "solemnly swear or affirm to support the Constitution of the United States" before assuming their duties. This legal requirement has lasted more than 200 years; even today, no Government employee may start work without taking an oath.

The First Amendment guarantees citizens the right to petition the Government. Nineteenth-century Americans believed it was their moral and civic duty to exercise this right—especially on controversial issues such as temperance, women's rights, and slavery.

From the 1830s through the Civil War, antislavery societies organized huge petition drives demanding that Congress abolish slavery and stop the spread of the slave trade. The petitions circulated through northern communities, often carried door to door by antislavery advocates. As the controversy over slavery grew, the petitions became more numerous and more urgent.

**Petition from women of Pennsylvania, 1844**
*National Archives, Records of the U.S. Senate*

In 1844, sixty-five Philadelphia women signed and presented to Congress this petition urging the abolition of slavery. At that time, women in the United States were unable to vote. To make their voices heard on the important social issues of their day—including slavery and drunkenness—women organized themselves and used petitions to influence Congress.

To the Senate and House of Representatives of the United States.

The undersigned, women of Pennsylvania, respectfully ask, that you will abolish every thing in the constitution or laws of the United States, which in any manner sanctions or sustains slavery.

As instruments of diplomacy, treaties protect and promote the interests of nations. Each country entering into an international agreement usually maintains a copy and gives a signed and sealed exchange copy to other parties to the agreement.

In keeping with their importance, early treaties were often highly decorative. They were bound in fine leather or rich fabrics and adorned with gold or silver coats of arms, tassels, and wax seals. Often a small round box called a skippet—which held a wax impression of the nation's or monarch's seal—was attached with silk or metallic cords.

Owing to their high cost, the Federal Government in 1871 put an end to the use of skippets; by 1920 other ornamentation was also discontinued.

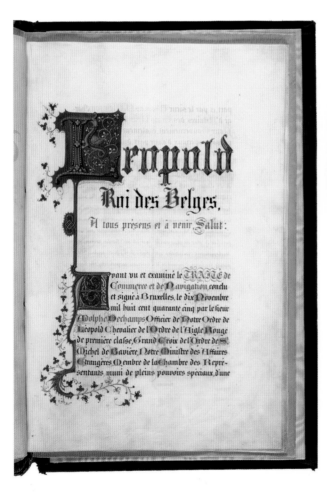

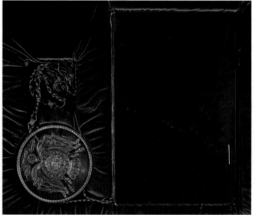

**Treaty of Commerce and Navigation between the United States and the Kingdom of Belgium, ratified March 30, 1846**
*National Archives, General Records of the U.S. Government*

A velvet binding protects the first treaty between the United States and the Kingdom of Belgium. The agreement, which established commerce and navigation conditions advantageous to both countries, was signed by King Leopold I on November 10, 1845. His signature was authenticated with a silver disk, or skippet, containing a wax seal with the Royal Arms of Belgium.

The Constitution mandates that every ten years the Federal Government take a census—a count of the number of people living in each and every residence across the country. The headcount is used to determine the number of members of the House of Representatives.

Early censuses simply listed heads of household and others living in the same dwelling. But in 1850, for the first time, censuses listed individuals instead of families, and census enumerators were charged with asking questions of residents—about place of birth, age, and occupation.

The data was recorded on forms called census schedules. Over centuries, the wealth of information in the schedules has been used by economists, historians, genealogists, and many other researchers.

Microfilmed copies of census schedules from 1790 through 1930 are available at the National Archives in Washington, DC, and its regional facilities. By law, information about individuals in census schedules is closed for seventy-two years after the census date.

**Census schedule for Concord, Massachusetts, 1850**
*National Archives, Records of the Bureau of the Census*

Line 33 of this census schedule from 1850 reveals that Henry David Thoreau—the author of *Walden*—was 33 years old and living at home with his parents in Concord, Massachusetts. Other volumes of the 1850 census from Massachusetts show well-known early-American writers Louisa May Alcott in Boston, Emily Dickinson in Amherst, and Henry Wadsworth Longfellow in Cambridge.

**The Emancipation Proclamation,**
**January 1, 1863**
Page 1 and signature page
*National Archives, General*
*Records of the U.S. Government*

opposite page:
**detail, signature page**

President Abraham Lincoln issued the Emancipation Proclamation on January 1, 1863, as the nation approached its third year of bloody civil war. The proclamation declared "that all persons held as slaves" within the rebellious states "are, and henceforward shall be free."

Despite Lincoln's expansive wording, the Emancipation Proclamation was limited in many ways. It applied only to states that had seceded from the Union, leaving slavery untouched in the loyal border states. It expressly exempted parts of the Confederacy that had already come under Union control. Most important, the freedom it promised depended upon Union military victory.

While the Emancipation Proclamation did not immediately free a single slave, it fundamentally transformed the character of the war. After January 1, 1863, every advance of Federal troops expanded the domain of freedom. Moreover, the liberated became liberators, for the proclamation announced the acceptance of black men into the Union army and navy. By the end of the war, nearly 200,000 black soldiers and sailors had fought for the Union and freedom.

The Emancipation Proclamation added moral force to the Union cause and strengthened the Union militarily and politically. As a milestone along the road to slavery's final destruction, the Emancipation Proclamation has assumed a place among the great documents of human freedom.

Abraham Lincoln was the first President to direct armed forces from Washington, DC. During the Civil War he used the relatively new technology of the telegraph to stay in contact with his commanders in the field and monitor the progress of battles.

Often working out of the War Department, the President wrote each message on telegraph stationery. A telegrapher then transmitted the words in Morse code to its destination, where another telegrapher received the message. Sometimes the telegrapher encountered problems, and communication would take an entire day to travel from Washington to the Virginia front line.

**Telegram from Abraham Lincoln to General Grant, February 1, 1865**
*National Archives, Records of the Office of the Secretary of War*

On February 1, 1865, President Lincoln sent this telegram to Gen. Ulysses S. Grant at City Point, Virginia, encouraging Grant to continue fighting vigorously: "Lieut[enant] Gen[eral] Grant, City Point. Let nothing which is transpiring, change, hinder, or delay your military movements or plans." Lincoln was about to meet with a Confederate peace delegation at Fort Monroe, Virginia, but he did not want the ongoing peace negotiations to prevent Grant from conducting offensive operations if the situation warranted.

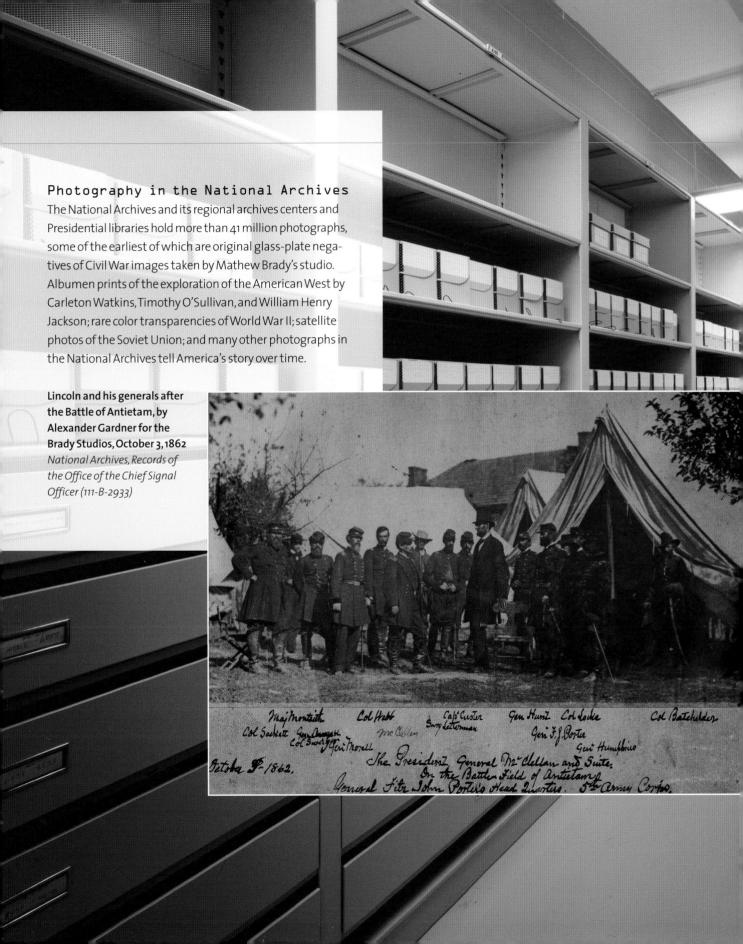

## Photography in the National Archives

The National Archives and its regional archives centers and Presidential libraries hold more than 41 million photographs, some of the earliest of which are original glass-plate negatives of Civil War images taken by Mathew Brady's studio. Albumen prints of the exploration of the American West by Carleton Watkins, Timothy O'Sullivan, and William Henry Jackson; rare color transparencies of World War II; satellite photos of the Soviet Union; and many other photographs in the National Archives tell America's story over time.

**Lincoln and his generals after the Battle of Antietam, by Alexander Gardner for the Brady Studios, October 3, 1862**
*National Archives, Records of the Office of the Chief Signal Officer (111-B-2933)*

Today, Government forms are commonplace. But when Abraham Lincoln signed the Homestead Act on May 20, 1862, they were something of a novelty. The Homestead Act offered 160 acres of land to those who lived on a property for five years and submitted proof of improvements, including a house and cultivation. To support their claims, homesteaders filled out some of the first standard forms issued by the U.S. Government. Homestead forms are a great resource for genealogists. They contain the name, age, address, and naturalization status of the applicant as well as children's names and birth dates.

**"Covered Wagon of the Great Western Migration, 1886, in Loup Valley, Nebraska," by Solomon D. Butcher, 1886**
*National Archives, Records of the Works Progress Administration (69-N-13606)*

## HOMESTEAD PROOF---TESTIMONY OF CLAIMANT.

*Almanzo J Wilder* being called as a witness in his own behalf in support of Homestead entry No. _____ for NE¼ 21-111-56 testifies as follows:

Ques. 1—What is your name (written in full and correctly spelled) your age and postoffice address?

Ans. *Almanzo J. Wilder.* 26 yrs old *DeSmet. Dakota*

Ques. 2—Are you a native of the United States, or have you been naturalized?

Ans. *Native citizen of US.*

Ques. 3—When was your house built on the land and when did you establish actual residence thereon? (Describe house and other improvements which you have placed on the land, giving total value thereof.)

Ans. *In September 1879. Residence same time. House 12 ft. square frame. 2 door 1 window. Cellar 2 wells for water. 2 stables 14×16 + 16×32 ft both frame. Some tree. 32 acres cultivation Value. over 300⁰⁰*

Ques. 4—Of whom does your family consist; and have you and your family resided continuously on the land since first establishing residence thereon? (If unmarried state the fact.)

Ans. *Am Single Man. Residence Continuous*

Ques. 5—For what period or periods have you been absent from the homestead since making settlement, and for what purpose; and if temporarily absent, did your family reside upon and cultivate the land during such absence?

Ans. *Was absent part of winter of 79 + 80. + temporarily for short times after at work on R.R. not more than a month at a time. absence was necessary for me to get money to improve my land.*

Ques. 6—How much of the land have you cultivated and for how many seasons have you raised crops thereon?

Ans. *32 acres cultivated now. Crops 4. yrs. 20 acres this season.*

Ques. 7—Are there any indications of coal, salines, or minerals of any kind on the land, and is the land more valuable for agricultural than for mineral purposes?

Ans. *No. No. No. more valuable for agriculture.*

Ques. 8—Have you ever made any other homestead entry? (If so, describe the same.)

Ans. *No*

Ques. 9—Have you sold, conveyed or mortgaged any portion of the land, and if so, to whom and for what purpose?

Ans. *No . No . No .*

*Almanzo, J. Wilder*

I Hereby Certify that the foregoing testimony was read to the claimant before being subscribed, and was sworn to before me this 12 day of September 1884

*W J Barnes*
*+ ex officio clerk*
Judge of Probate
COURT
KINGSBURY CO, DAK.

(SEE NOTE ON FOURTH PAGE.)

**Homestead form of Almanzo J. Wilder, 1884**

*National Archives, Records of the Bureau of Land Management*

This document from 1884 records the sworn statements of Almanzo Wilder that he had built a "12 ft. square frame" house in the Dakota Territory and was cultivating the land. Wilder had established the 160-acre homestead five years earlier, through the Homestead Act. It was his first home with his wife, Laura Ingalls Wilder, who many years later would write *Little House on the Prairie* and other novels for children about pioneer life.

You've come up with a brilliant idea and you don't want anyone to copy it. What do you do? Apply for a patent, which protects authors and inventors by giving them exclusive rights to their writings and discoveries for a limited time. The Constitution empowers Congress to grant these limited monopolies.

The Patent Act of 1790 established the rules for submitting an application. Each applicant had to provide written specifications, a patent drawing, and—if possible—a model of the invention. Eventually, models were no longer required.

The National Archives holds nearly 3 million patent case files dating from 1836 to 1956. They offer a window into the ingenuity and imagination of individuals and the nation.

**Patent drawing for "Electric-Lamp" (light bulb), by Thomas Edison, 1880**
*National Archives, Records of the Patent and Trademark Office*

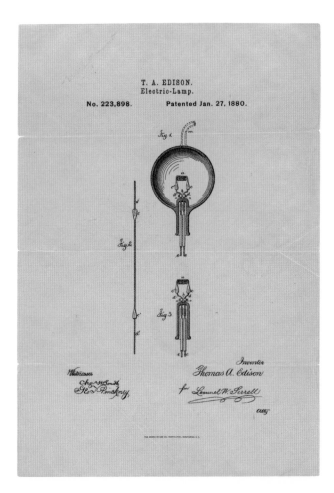

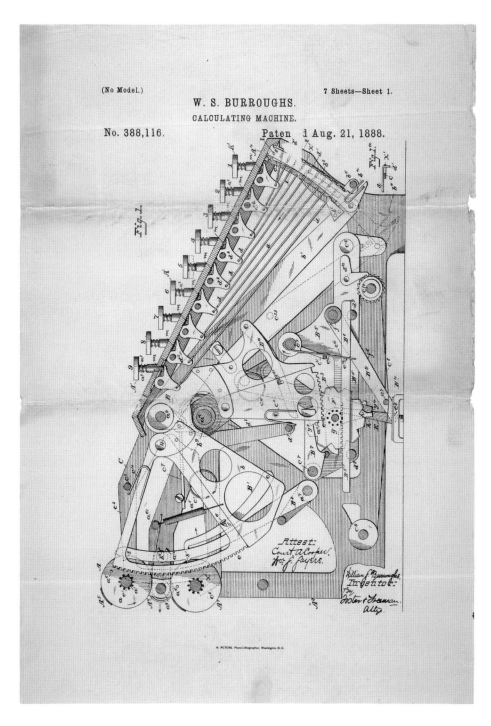

**Patent drawing for "Calculating Machine," by William Seward Burroughs, 1888**
*National Archives, Records of the Patent and Trademark Office*

This drawing by William Seward Burroughs is from his first patent application for a calculating machine—an important step toward the modern computer. A sometime clerk, box maker, and mechanic, Burroughs resolved to invent a machine that could add automatically and print the result. He was issued the patent on August 21, 1888.

# SHIP PASSENGER ARRIVAL RECORD

Any person who has legally entered the United States by ship since 1820 may be listed on a ship's passenger record. Passenger manifests have been required since the Act Regulating Passenger Vessels of 1819 sought to protect those onboard from overcrowding and provide a basis for immigration statistics. Early lists recorded each passenger's name, age, sex, occupation, and nationality, but stricter immigration laws after 1875 called for more data. By the early twentieth century, a ship's passenger arrival record included information about each immigrant's home, destination, health, literacy, and criminal or political behavior.

Passenger lists survive for New York City as well as for other ports of entry such as San Francisco and New Orleans. The National Archives holds hundreds of thousands of microfilmed copies of ship passenger arrival lists from 1820 to about 1954, and microfilmed passenger records are available at National Archives' facilities nationwide.

**Immigrants on a ferry boat near Ellis Island, ca. 1920**
*National Archives, Records of the Public Health Service (90-G-125-6)*

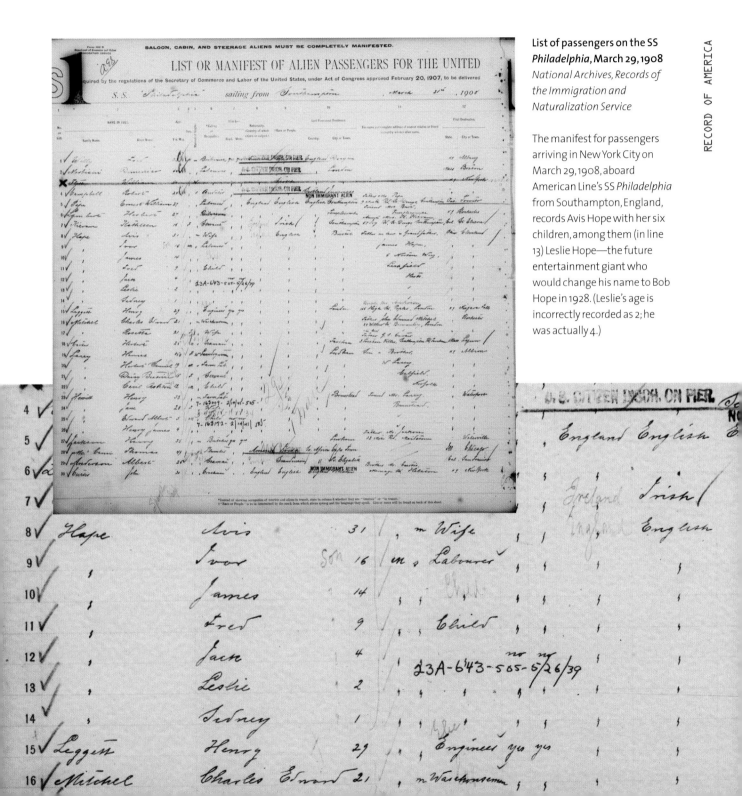

**List of passengers on the SS *Philadelphia*, March 29, 1908**
*National Archives, Records of the Immigration and Naturalization Service*

The manifest for passengers arriving in New York City on March 29, 1908, aboard American Line's SS *Philadelphia* from Southampton, England, records Avis Hope with her six children, among them (in line 13) Leslie Hope—the future entertainment giant who would change his name to Bob Hope in 1928. (Leslie's age is incorrectly recorded as 2; he was actually 4.)

Audio recordings capture life with a unique immediacy. Historic news broadcasts; Presidents' speeches, Presidential press conferences, and White House conversations; oral histories; court proceedings; arts and entertainment; and more are brought back to life through recordings. Among the earliest media for sound recording are wax cylinders, which were made by a needle that cut grooves in wax.

Technology has advanced exponentially since the days of wax cylinders. Succeeding generations have listened to sound on acetate, shellac, and vinyl discs; on wire and Dictaphone recordings; on cassette and reel-to-reel tapes. Today we use digital media. Whatever the original technology, audio technicians at the National Archives are able to make copies that enable researchers and others to experience rare and historical recordings and be transported back to a moment in time.

**Theodore Roosevelt speaking to a crowd, ca. 1917**
*National Archives, Records of the War Department, General and Special Staffs
(165-WW-420-P237)*

## Wax-Cylinder Recording

Wax cylinders, invented by Thomas Edison, represent the earliest form of sound recordings in the National Archives. Audio technicians in National Archives' laboratories make copies using modern devices built specifically for cylinder playback—allowing researchers and visitors to experience rare historical recordings.

One such recording is Theodore Roosevelt's speech, "The Progressive Party's Movement for Social and Industrial Justice." The former Republican President joined the Progressive Party and launched his "Bull Moose" campaign for the Presidency in 1912; he won 27 percent of the popular vote but lost to Democrat Woodrow Wilson.

"We stand for the rights of the people. We stand for the rights of the wageworker. We stand for his right to a living wage. We stand for the right and duty of the Government to limit the hours of women in industry. To abolish child labor. To shape the conditions of life and living so that the average wageworker shall be able so to lead his own life, and so to support his wife and his children. That these children shall grow up into men and women fit for the exacting duties of American citizenship."

Theodore Roosevelt

Container for a wax-cylinder recording of Theodore Roosevelt, ca. 1912
*Donated Materials in the National Archives*

During World War I many branches of the Federal Government distributed posters to urge Americans to support the war effort. In a world without radio, television, or the Internet, posters were a cheap way to deliver powerful messages to millions—to buy liberty bonds, join the armed forces, or conserve food and natural resources. Well-known artists created designs that summoned patriotism and unified the American people. Like congressional broadsides from an earlier era, World War I posters were hung in public places, such as post offices, schools, factories, recruiting stations, and private homes. The National Archives holds more than 18,000 posters produced by civilian and military agencies.

THAT LIBERTY SHALL NOT PERISH FROM THE EARTH
BUY LIBERTY BONDS
FOURTH LIBERTY LOAN

**"That Liberty Shall Not Perish from the Earth," poster by Joseph Pennell, 1918**
*National Archives, Records of the Bureau of Public Debt (53-WP-2B)*

The German air and submarine attack depicted by Joseph Pennell in this 1918 poster never actually took place. By evoking a potential threat, however, the image brought the war home to the American people and underlined the urgency of buying bonds during Liberty Loan drives. The Government printed 2 million copies of this enormously popular poster.

## FDR's FIRESIDE CHAT

A masterful communicator, President Franklin D. Roosevelt directly reached millions of Americans through informal radio addresses. He used these opportunities to outline his policies and urge support of his programs. Reporters called the addresses "fireside chats" because they made listeners feel that the President was talking with them personally. During his twelve years in office, Roosevelt gave thirty-one fireside chats, each lasting approximately thirty minutes.

On March 12, 1933, thousands of banks were failing, and millions of Americans feared losing their savings. Faced with a crisis in public confidence, President Roosevelt used his first fireside chat to explain why he had proclaimed a bank "holiday" and when the Federal Government would allow the banks to reopen. The broadcast reached an estimated 60 million people.

All but three of FDR's fireside chats were recorded directly onto glass recording disks. Recordings of twenty-eight fireside chats are preserved by the Franklin D. Roosevelt Library in Hyde Park, New York.

**Farmer listening to the radio, Clarkston, Utah, August 1933**
*National Archives, Records of the Office of the Secretary of Agriculture (16-G-93-2-S17878C)*

opposite page:
**Text of fireside chat on the banking crisis, March 12, 1933**
Page 1
*National Archives, Franklin D. Roosevelt Library*

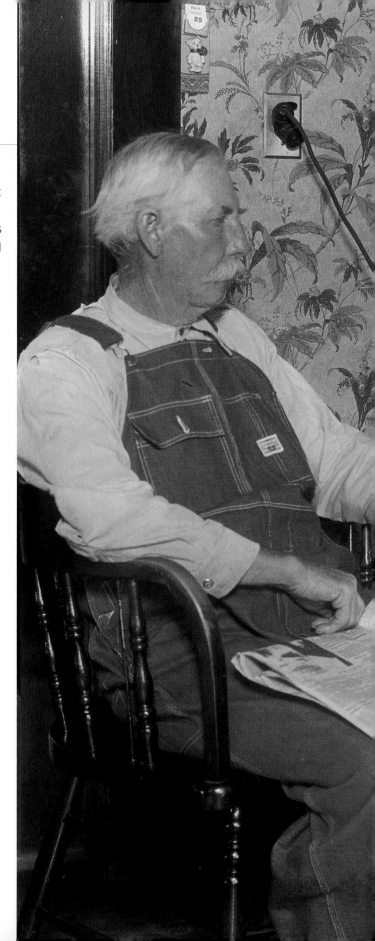

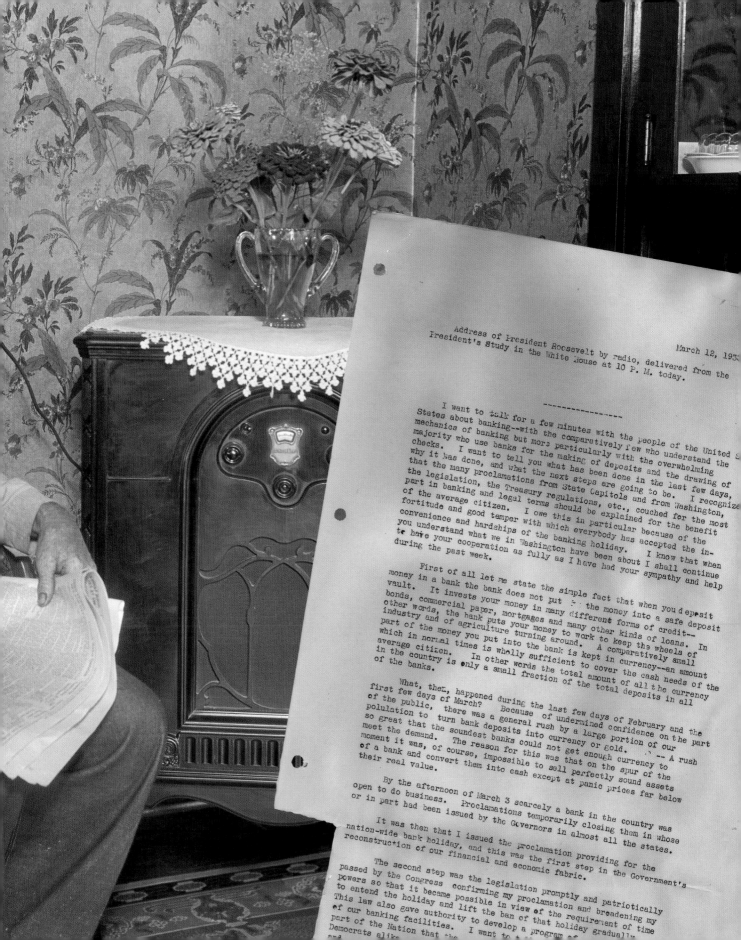

March 12, 1933

Address of President Roosevelt by radio, delivered from the
President's study in the White House at 10 P. M. today.

------------------

I want to talk for a few minutes with the people of the United S___
States about banking--with the comparatively few who understand the
mechanics of banking but more particularly with the overwhelming
majority who use banks for the making of deposits and the drawing of
checks. I want to tell you what has been done in the last few days,
why it was done, and what the next steps are going to be. I recognize
that the many proclamations from State Capitols and from Washington,
the legislation, the Treasury regulations, etc., couched for the most
part in banking and legal terms should be explained for the benefit
of the average citizen. I owe this in particular because of the
fortitude and good temper with which everybody has accepted the in-
convenience and hardships of the banking holiday. I know that when
you understand what we in Washington have been about I shall continue
to have your cooperation as fully as I have had your sympathy and help
during the past week.

First of all let me state the simple fact that when you deposit
money in a bank the bank does not put _ _ the money into a safe deposit
vault. It invests your money in many different forms of credit--
bonds, commercial paper, mortgages and many other kinds of loans. In
other words, the bank puts your money to work to keep the wheels of
industry and of agriculture turning around. A comparatively small
part of the money you put into the bank is kept in currency--an amount
which in normal times is wholly sufficient to cover the cash needs of the
average citizen. In other words the total amount of all the currency
in the country is only a small fraction of the total deposits in all
of the banks.

What, then, happened during the last few days of February and the
first few days of March? Because of undermined confidence on the part
of the public, there was a general rush by a large portion of our
population to turn bank deposits into currency or gold. _ _ _ -- A rush
so great that the soundest banks could not get enough currency to
meet the demand. The reason for this was that on the spur of the
moment it was, of course, impossible to sell perfectly sound assets
of a bank and convert them into cash except at panic prices far below
their real value.

By the afternoon of March 3 scarcely a bank in the country was
open to do business. Proclamations temporarily closing them in whose
or in part had been issued by the Governors in almost all the states.

It was then that I issued the proclamation providing for the
nation-wide bank holiday, and this was the first step in the Government's
reconstruction of our financial and economic fabric.

The second step was the legislation promptly and patriotically
passed by the Congress confirming my proclamation and broadening my
powers so that it became possible in view of the requirement of time
to entend the holiday and lift the ban of that holiday gradually.
This law also gave authority to develop a program of _ _ _ _
part of the Nation that the _ _
Democrats alike _ _

Throughout its history the Federal Government has overseen thousands of construction projects of different sizes and designs. Think of the Washington Monument, Federal courthouses around the nation, indeed, the National Archives Building in Washington, DC, and all the Presidential libraries and regional facilities it directs. Federal buildings existed on paper as drawings, design specifications, and blueprints before they were transformed from idea to reality. The National Archives holds more than 3 million architectural and engineering plans for structures ranging from bridges to barracks, monuments to museums, prisons to post offices. This wealth of graphic information helps architectural historians understand why and how buildings were built and enables preservationists to restore and rehabilitate historic structures.

**Alcatraz prison, not dated**
*National Archives, Records of the Bureau of Prisons (129-G-175-1)*

Situated on an island in San Francisco Bay, the U.S. Penitentiary on Alcatraz was a military prison before it became a civilian maximum-security penitentiary. For thirty-four years it held some of the nation's toughest criminals, including Al Capone and "Machine Gun" Kelly. Robert Stroud, more familiarly known as the Birdman of Alcatraz, served eleven of his seventeen years in the prison hospital shown in this architectural plan from 1940. Today Alcatraz is one of the Bay area's most popular tourist destinations.

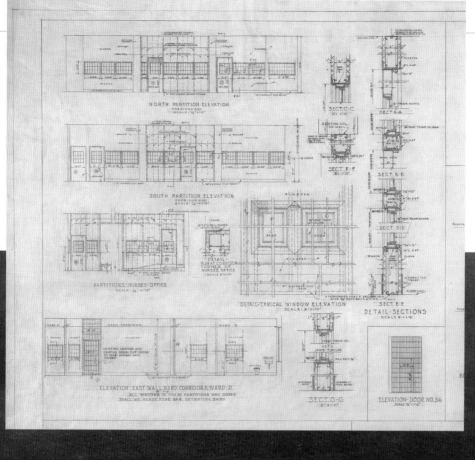

left:

**Detail from Alcatraz architectural drawing, "Modernization of Hospital, Miscellaneous Details," May 25, 1940**

*National Archives, Records of the Public Buildings Service*

Every four hours, using the navy's special language and procedures, officers aboard U.S. naval vessels make notations in a deck log to describe what has transpired. Ships "c/c" (change course) or "c/s" (change speed). Distances are measured in "yds" (yards), depths in "ft" (feet). Speed is recorded in "kts" (knots), direction in "°T" (degrees true). "S.O.P.A." is the Senior Officer Present Afloat. The watch officer signs the entries for each four-hour period, and the ship's navigator and commanding officer approve each day's entries.

Most activities aboard ship are routine. Sometimes, however, an event changes the course of history, and the document that records it marks a milestone. Together with photographs, film, action reports, and war diaries, navy log books are critical tools that help historians re-create events as thoroughly and accurately as possible.

**Deck log of the USS *Missouri*,
September 2, 1945**
*National Archives, Records of
the Bureau of Naval Personnel*

This page from the deck log of the USS *Missouri* for September 2, 1945, reports preparations for the surrender of Japan to the Allied powers, which ended World War II. The surrender proceedings themselves are summarized in the entry for the hours 8 A.M. to noon. The log book's next entry records the times when every party signed the document.

main image:
**The USS *Missouri*,
September 2, 1945**
*National Archives, General
Records of the Department of
the Navy, 1798–1947
(80-6-700770)*

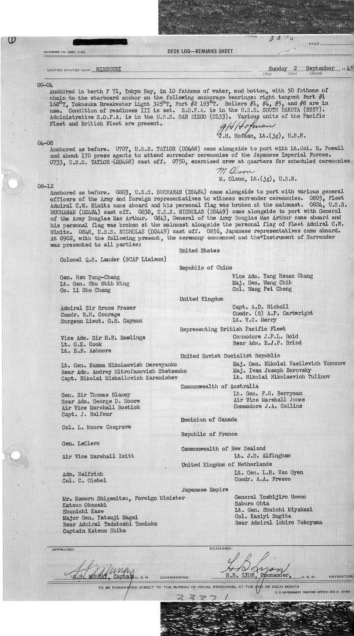

Today digital television presents Presidential speeches in startlingly lifelike picture and sound, and we are accustomed to seeing the President on television almost daily. That was not always the case.

In 1939, Franklin D. Roosevelt became the first President seen on television, thirteen years after the first public demonstration of the fledgling media. On October 5, 1947, when President Harry S. Truman delivered the first televised Presidential address—on the subject of the international food crisis—more than 44,000 television sets were in use in the United States.

Ten years later, when President Dwight D. Eisenhower delivered a speech from the Oval Office in response to the crisis surrounding desegregation of schools in Little Rock, Arkansas, almost 80 percent of American households had televisions. The National Archives and its Presidential libraries hold thousands of hours of televised Presidential speeches, addresses, and proclamations.

**President Dwight D. Eisenhower preparing for a nationally broadcast press conference, February 29, 1956**
*National Archives, Dwight D. Eisenhower Library*
*(72-1629-2)*

opposite page:
**Text for President Eisenhower's Little Rock Crisis speech (third draft), September 24, 1957**
Page 1
*National Archives, Dwight D. Eisenhower Library*

President Dwight D. Eisenhower delivered this speech from the Oval Office at 9 P.M. on September 24, 1957. Arkansas Governor Orval Faubus had just defied the Supreme Court's *Brown* v. *Topeka Board of Education* decision to desegregate schools. In this address, Eisenhower announced his response: he was deploying troops to desegregate Little Rock's Central High School.

My Fellow Citizens:

For a few minutes I ~~would like~~ *want* to speak to you about the

serious -- indeed the sad -- situation which has arisen in Little Rock.

In that city, under the ~~premediated~~ leadership of demagogic extremists,

*Deliberately*

disorderly mobs have prevented the carrying out of proper orders of a

*Local authorities have not succeeded*

Federal Court acting ~~in conformity with the requirements of the Con~~
*in eliminating that orders of parties and,*
~~stitution of the United States.~~ *under the law, I yesterday issued a*
*proclamation calling upon the mob to disperse.*
*This morning the mob again gathered in front*

When it becomes necessary for the Executive Branch of the
*even*

Federal Government of this nation to use its powers and authority to uphold

*The President's*

Federal Courts ~~my~~ responsibility is *inescapable* ~~clear.~~

I have today issued an Executive Order authorizing and directing
*under Federal authority*
the use of ~~Federal~~ troops to aid in the execution of the law at Little Rock,

*became* *when*
Arkansas. This ~~was~~ necessary ~~because~~ my Proclamation of yesterday

~~calling upon all persons in the are to refrain from obstructing justice~~ was

not observed. Indeed, the situation has progressively worsened. ~~Con-~~

~~sequently, no reasonable choice remained open to me.~~

It is important that the reasons for my action be completely clear

and fully understood.. *and change unconstitutional*

As you know, the Supreme Court of the United States has declared

that separate educational facilities for the races are inherently unequal.

*Our personal opinions as to the accuracy of*
*the decision have no bearing on the matter;*
*the authority responsible of the Supreme Court to*
*interpret the constitution is unquestioned.*

# SATELLITE IMAGE

During the Cold War the United States literally went to outer space to gather intelligence, and the satellite became an important tool for collecting information about developments in the Communist world. In 1960 the CORONA project, a classified program run by the CIA and the Air Force, produced the first satellite images with a series of cameras known as KEYHOLE. As satellites improved, so did cameras, lenses, and film. Data transmission was soon real-time, and resolution was in feet. The CORONA program ended in 1972 after producing more than 800,000 satellite photos.

While the function of the first reconnaissance satellites was primarily for military use and intelligence, today commercial satellites are available for a variety of purposes, including communications, mapping, archaeology, and environmental uses. The National Archives holds nearly 1 million satellite images.

**Titan III rocket lifting off from the launch pad at Cape Kennedy, Florida, July 14, 1969**
*National Archives, Records of U.S. Air Force Commands, Activities, and Organizations (342-B-02-017-1-KE53799)*

**Moscow from space, May 28, 1970**
*National Archives, Records of the Central Intelligence Agency*

On May 28, 1970, a CORONA satellite, using two cameras, took this photograph of Moscow (represented here by the negative, at right, and a print, on opposite page). The exposed film was then stored in canisters, de-orbited, and retrieved by aircraft in midair. Inside the two boxes in the print are enlargements of the Kremlin.

To organize information collected as part of their missions, Government agencies routinely create electronic databases. The vastness of the information can be astounding. While the databases are produced for particular purposes, their versatility allows researchers to find new uses for the data over time.

The National Archives preserves billions of electronic records—from census records to Presidential e-mails—and is responsible for maintaining records and making them available to the public, regardless of the technology used. Electronic records present a new challenge to the preservation and access of records. National Archives staff must find ways to provide continued access to databases as technology changes and software and hardware become outdated.

A selection of databases can be searched online at *www.archives.gov.*

**VIETNAM P.O.W. DATABASE**

**DATABASE RECORD**

NAME
**KROBOTH ALAN JOSEPH**

| SEX | AGE | DATE OF BIRTH | HOME CITY/STATE | CITIZEN |
|-----|-----|---------------|-----------------|---------|
| Male | 25 | 1947-12-23 | LINDEN, New Jersey | U.S. |

| RACE | RELIGION | MARITAL STATUS | SOCIAL SECURITY OR SERVICE NUMBER |
|------|----------|----------------|-----------------------------------|
| Caucasian | ## | Married (Spouse Listed) | ### ### #### |

| MILITARY SERVICE | COMPONENT | REFERENCE NUMBER |
|------------------|-----------|------------------|
| United States Marine Corps | Regular (RA, USN, USAF, USMC, USCG) | 193 |

| MILITARY GRADE | PAY GRADE | SERVICE OCCUPATION |
|----------------|-----------|--------------------|
| FIRST LIEUTENANT | O2 | Pilot |

| TYPE OF CASUALTY | COUNTRY OF CASUALTY |
|------------------|---------------------|
| Hostile - Captured/Interned - Returned to Military Control | Republic of Vietnam (South Vietnam) |

| DATE RELEASED OR RETURNED | REASON | AIRCRAFT OR NOT AIRCRAFT |
|---------------------------|--------|--------------------------|
| 1973-03-27 | Aircraft Loss/Crash Not at Sea | Fixed Wing Air Casualty - Other Aircrew |

| POSTHUMOUS PROMOTION | LENGTH OF SERVICE IN YEARS | DATE TOUR IN SOUTHEAST ASIA BEGAN |
|----------------------|----------------------------|-----------------------------------|
| Not Posthumously Promoted | * | * |

| BODY RECOVERED OR NOT | DATE RECORD PROCESSED | COMMENTS |
|-----------------------|------------------------|----------|
| Null | 1973-03 | |

NEW SEARCH          NEXT →

Some information marked with * is unknown, other information has been marked with # for privacy reasons.

**Information from the Vietnam War POW Database**
*National Archives, Records of the Office of the Secretary of Defense*

As missing or captured soldiers were returned during the Vietnam War, the information was recorded electronically in the "Combat Casualities Returned Alive File," part of the Combat Area Casualties Data Base created by the Office of the Secretary of Defense. Using the National Archives web site, *www.archives.gov,* individuals can search the entire database, including the more than 700 names of POWs returned alive after the war.

above:
**Operation Homecoming, February 12, 1973**
*National Archives, Records of the U.S. Marine Corps (127-N-A900089)*

The arrival of the World Wide Web in the early 1990s provided a new way for the Federal Government to serve the people. Today, Federal agencies—including the White House—maintain one or more web sites, offering services and an enormous amount of information. The worldwide network of computers known as the Internet was conceived in the 1960s as a U.S. Department of Defense communication network. The World Wide Web greatly expanded Internet use by enabling users to link to resources organized by colorful, graphic-oriented web pages. The National Archives helps Federal agencies manage their web records, preserves snapshots of web sites, and offers access to many resources and services through *www.archives.gov*.

A first for a President was established on October 20, 1994, when the Clinton administration unveiled the first White House web site—*Welcome to the White House: An Interactive Citizens' Handbook*. Internet users could search for information about the First Family, find links to executive branch departments and agencies, and send messages to the President and Vice President. The site was revised five times between 1994 and 2001.

**Surfing the first Presidential web site**
*National Archives, William J. Clinton Library*

# WE THE PEOPLE
## RECORDS OF FAMILIES AND CITIZENSHIP

Alongside the stories of the great and powerful, millions of records give insight into the lives of ordinary people. Nearly all Americans can find themselves, their neighbors, their ancestors, or their community in the collections of the National Archives, which holds records not just for the Government but also for individuals and families. Among these are photographs of families; birth, death, and naturalization records; marriage licenses; and other records that document family histories or identify American citizenship. The types of records found in this section are often used by ordinary citizens to connect to their roots and get a richer understanding of their place in the pageant of American history.

clockwise from top: **George and Linda Galvin family, Oxnard, California, attributed to Tom Kasser, ca. 1982**, *National Archives, Records of the U.S. Information Agency (306-PSE-82-524);* **Unidentified family, Spartanburg County, South Carolina, by E. F. Shipp, September 12, 1928,** *National Archives, Records of the Office of the Secretary of Agriculture (16-G-162[1][S11316C]);* **Unidentified family,** *National Archives, Records of the Public Buildings Service (121-BA-230-A);*

**Fisherman's family, Lake Pontchartrain, Louisiana, by John Messina, July 1972,** *National Archives, Records of the Environmental Protection Agency (412-DA-1692)*

overleaf:
**Lee Wai She and children, Honolulu, Hawaii, 1913,** *National Archives—Pacific Region (San Bruno), Records of the Immigration and Naturalization Service (2989-C)*

ENTER>

Revolutionary War veterans and their families submitted hundreds of documents to support claims for pensions based on their service to the nation. Pension records include family histories in a variety of formats that chronicle births, baptisms, marriages, and deaths. Even family trees were saved as evidence. Some of these family histories are beautifully illustrated with decorative elements, whether printed or hand-drawn. One type of illustrated family record, commonly bearing bird and leaf motifs, is the fraktur. Created by and for members of the Pennsylvania Dutch culture, frakturs typically were written in German using a German script. A few cloth samplers recording family history are also preserved in the National Archives.

**Illustrated family record from file of Jacob Esser, Pennsylvania, ca. 1810–15**
*National Archives, Records of the Veterans Administration*

This fraktur, or illustrated family record, records the birth and baptism (*Geburts und Taufscheine*) of Jacob Esser, son of Jacob and Anna. Esser submitted the fraktur with his application for a land warrant based upon his Revolutionary War service. Notice the winged creatures in the upper left and right corners. They appear in frakturs attributed to an artist identified only as the Flying Angel Artist.

opposite page:
**Illustrated family record from the file of Isaac Dickisson, New Jersey, ca. 1845**
*National Archives, Records of the Veterans Administration*

How does a person from another country become an American?

An immigrant becomes an American citizen—or is naturalized—by going through an extended process. Congress passed the first naturalization act in 1790. For many years, naturalization took five years. Two years after establishing a residence in the United States, an applicant would file in any court a declaration of intention to become a citizen. The declaration informed the Government that he or she renounced allegiance to all foreign sovereignty and intended to become a citizen.

Three years later, the candidate for citizenship would take the second step by filing a petition for naturalization. If the court granted the petition, the applicant received a certificate of citizenship. At various times, exceptions applied to the general rule. One allowed for derivative citizenship to be granted to wives and children of naturalized men. Other exceptions permitted a minor to file a declaration and petition at the same time, and a veteran to become a citizen without filing a declaration.

A rich resource for family history, millions of these forms are now in the National Archives, mostly within the records of the U.S. District Courts housed in the National Archives' regional facilities.

TRIPLICATE
(To be given to declarant)

No. 1442

# UNITED STATES OF AMERICA

## DECLARATION OF INTENTION
(Invalid for all purposes seven years after the date hereof)

United States of America
District of New Jersey } ss:

In the _____ District _____ Court
of The United States at Trenton, N. J.

I, _____ Dr. Albert Einstein _____
now residing at 112 Mercer St., (full true name, without abbreviation, and any other name which has been used, most spelling) Princeton (City or town) Mercer (County) N.J. (State)
occupation Professor, aged 56 years, do declare on oath that my personal description is:
Sex Male, color White, complexion Fair, color of eyes Brown
color of hair Grey, height 5 feet 7 inches; weight 175 pounds; visible distinctive marks
none
race Hebrew; nationality German
I was born in Ulm (City or town), Germany (Country), on March 14 (Month) (Day) 1879 (Year)
I am married. The name of my wife or husband is Elsa; she or he was
we were married on April 6th 1917, at Berlin, Germany (State or country); she or he was
born at Hechingen, Germany (State or country), on January 18, 1877, entered the United States
at New York (City or town) N.Y. (State), on June 3 1935 (Year), for permanent residence therein, and now
resides at with me. I have 2 children, and the name, date and place of birth,
and place of residence of each of said children are as follows: Albert born 5-14-1905 and
Eduard born 6-28-1910 both born and reside in Switzerland

I have not heretofore made a declaration of intention: Number _____, on _____ (Date)
at _____ (City or town)
my last foreign residence was Bermuda (City or town) Great Britain (Name of court)
I emigrated to the United States of America from Bermuda (City or town) Great Britain (Country)
my lawful entry for permanent residence in the United States was at New York (City or town) N.Y. (State)
under the name of Albert Einstein, on June 3, 1935 (Day) (Year)
on the vessel SS Queen of Bermuda (If other than by vessel, state manner of arrival)
I will, before being admitted to citizenship, renounce forever all allegiance and fidelity to any foreign prince, potentate, state, or sovereignty, and particularly, by name, to the prince, potentate, state, or sovereignty of which I may be at the time of admission a citizen or subject; I am not an anarchist; I am not a polygamist nor a believer in the practice of polygamy; and it is my intention in good faith to become a citizen of the United States of America and to reside permanently therein; and I certify that the photograph affixed to the duplicate and triplicate hereof is a likeness of me: So HELP ME GOD.

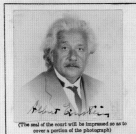

(The seal of the court will be impressed so as to cover a portion of the photograph)

*Albert Einstein*
(Original signature of declarant without abbreviation, also alias, if used)

Subscribed and sworn to before me in the office of the Clerk of said Court, at Trenton, N. J. this 15th day of January anno Domini 1936. Certification No. 3-180742 from the Commissioner of Immigration and Naturalization showing the lawful entry of the declarant for permanent residence on the date stated above, has been received by me. The photograph affixed to the duplicate and triplicate hereof is a likeness of the declarant.

George T. Cranmer
[SEAL] Clerk of the U. S. District Court.
By _____, Deputy Clerk.

Form 2202—L-A
U. S. DEPARTMENT OF LABOR
IMMIGRATION AND NATURALIZATION SERVICE

14—2623
U. S. GOVERNMENT PRINTING OFFICE: 1935

Nº 5773

---

**Declaration of intention for Albert Einstein, January 15, 1936**
*National Archives–Northeast Region (New York), Records of the District Courts of the United States*

Among the many declarations and petitions in the National Archives are those of immigrants who went on to achieve greatness or celebrity. Examination of their records—which often reveal original names, places of origin, and occupations—can lead to a new understanding of people we thought we knew. Albert Einstein, who won the Nobel Prize for physics in 1921, filed a declaration of intention in January 1936 after immigrating to the United States in 1933 to escape Nazi persecution.

opposite page:
**Federal Judge Michael Igoe administers the oath of allegiance to the United States to a group of new citizens, October 13, 1939**
*National Archives, Records of the U.S. Information Agency (306-PS-49-13909)*

# FIRST FAMILIES GROWING UP

The National Archives administers the Presidential library system, which holds records spanning the entire lives of modern Presidents since Herbert Hoover, the thirty-first President (1929–33). This nationwide network preserves and makes available the papers, records, and other historical materials of the Presidents; it also contains official memoranda and declassified documents as well as home movies and childhood photographs. The Presidential libraries are open to the public and found in cities and towns across America.

## The Presidential libraries are...

...Herbert Hoover Library, West Branch, Iowa; Franklin D. Roosevelt Library, Hyde Park, New York; Harry S. Truman Library, Independence, Missouri; Dwight D. Eisenhower Library, Abilene, Kansas; John F. Kennedy Library, Boston, Massachusetts; Lyndon Baines Johnson Library, Austin, Texas; Nixon Presidential Materials Project, College Park, Maryland; Gerald R. Ford Library, Ann Arbor, Michigan; Gerald R. Ford Museum, Grand Rapids, Michigan; Jimmy Carter Library, Atlanta, Georgia; Ronald Reagan Library, Simi Valley, California; George Bush Library, College Station, Texas; and William J. Clinton Library, Little Rock, Arkansas.

**The White House, 1992**
*George Bush Library*
*(P31020-06)*

## CAN YOU GUESS WHO'S WHO?

Match the Presidents and First Ladies named below to the photographs on the opposite page by placing the correct numbers in the boxes. (The answers are given below.)

☐ Franklin D. Roosevelt

☐ Harry S. Truman

☐ Gerald R. Ford

☐ Lou Henry Hoover

☐ Claudia Alta ("Lady Bird") Taylor Johnson

☐ Barbara Pierce Bush

1. Harry S. Truman, age 13, 1897
*National Archives, Harry S. Truman Library (79-26)*

2. Gerald R. Ford, about age 5
*National Archives, Gerald R. Ford Library (H0040.3)*

3. Claudia Alta ("Lady Bird") Taylor Johnson, age 3, 1915
*National Archives, Lyndon Baines Johnson Library (B-9742)*

4. Lou Henry Hoover, about age 17
*National Archives, Herbert Hoover Library (1891-5)*

5. Barbara Pierce Bush, age 7, 1932
*National Archives, George Bush Library (H011-28)*

6. Franklin D. Roosevelt, about age 11
*National Archives, Franklin D. Roosevelt Library (09-1957, 47961168)*

Before the Revolutionary War, some early Americans were already living in what is now U.S. territory. Others entered the country after 1787 as immigrants or slaves. But there was another way in which some people became American citizens: when the land they lived on was annexed, conquered, or purchased by the United States.

When the United States acquired new lands, residents faced decisions about their citizenship. Petitions, announcements, and legal cases document some of the transitions that occurred as the residents of newly acquired lands changed from neighbors to citizens and were granted the rights of citizenship.

**_Diseño_ drawing of land claim of Thomas Sanchez, 1852**
_National Archives, Records of the Bureau of Land Management_

The Mexican Cession of 1848 transferred 529,017 square miles of territory to the United States—along with jurisdiction over a legal battle for a league of land left by Vicente Sanchez, who died in 1846. This hand-drawn map, or _diseño_, of his ranch, together with a claim appealing the division of the land (also in the National Archives), was filed in 1852 with the California Land Commission. The commission eventually confirmed the division of the land between Sanchez's widow and a descendant.

Ytano del Rancho del paso de la tijera, con la estencion de un cho de ganado mayor

Lynderos de Vg.º Machado entre las Lomas

LYNDERO de la fuente de la Cristo

LYNDERO JANJA DEL RODEO DE ENMEDYO

CYENEGA

CYENEGA

LYNDERO, SANJON DE HAGUA DELA TYJERA

Escala de una milla

Established by Congress on March 3, 1865, the Bureau of Refugees, Freedmen, and Abandoned Lands assisted newly freed African Americans in making the transition from slavery to freedom. The Bureau arranged for food, shelter, schools, and medical care. It assisted freedmen with labor arrangements and secured justice for former slaves. The Bureau had more than 900 agents placed throughout the southern and border states and the District of Columbia.

During its short lifetime, the Freedmen's Bureau created a large volume of records that document the Bureau's activities and the histories of the families it served during Reconstruction. Among the records are reports on local schools, marriage certificates, applications for land, and labor contracts. As a vital link between former slaves and their descendants, Freedmen's Bureau records document a crucial time in the African American experience.

Store for Freedmen
Beaufort, S.C.

## Education

The Bureau facilitated the founding of nearly 3,000 schools for former slaves and their children. The records they created include reports on the conditions and progress in the schools.

**Teacher's Monthly School Report for Williams School in Virginia, September 1869**
*National Archives, Records of the Bureau of Refugees, Freedmen, and Abandoned Lands*

opposite page:
**"Store for Freedmen, Beaufort, South Carolina," by Sam A. Cooley, December 18, 1864**
*National Archives, Records of the War Department General and Special Staffs (165-C-393)*

[Ed. Form, No. 3.]

# TEACHER'S MONTHLY SCHOOL REPORT

### For the Month of *September*, 186*9*.

☞ To contain one entire calendar month, and to be forwarded as soon as possible after the close of the month.
☞ A School under the distinct control of one Teacher, or a Teacher with one Assistant, is to be reported as one School.

[Answers placed here.]

Name of your School? *Williams* *Sam A Form* Location (town, county, or district)? *Elizabeth*

Is it a Day or Night-School? *Day* Of what grade? *Grammar*

When did your present session commence? *Sept 1* When to close? *July 8th*

Is your School supported by an Educational Society? *No* What Society? *A.M.A.*

Is your School supported wholly by local School Board? *No* Name of Board or Com.? Am't pd. this month?

Is your School supported in part by local School Board? *No* Name of Board or Com.? Am't pd. this month?

Is your School supported wholly by Freedmen? *No* Amount paid this month? *$2.10*

Is your School supported in part by Freedmen? *Yes* Amount paid this month?

Have you had Bureau transportation this term? *No*

Who owns the School-building? *Guy Edwards*

Is rent paid by Freedmen's Bureau? *No* How much per month? *1*

What number of Teachers and Assistants in your School? *1* White? *1* Colored? *No I am a Negro*

Total enrolment for the month? † *37* Male? *20* Female? *17*

Number enrolled last report? *53* { Number enrolled last report, by adding new scholars and subtracting those left school, must equal the present total enrolment. }

Number left school this month? *16*

Number new Scholars this month? *8* { Schools are to be kept five days per week and six hours each day. }

What is the average attendance? *28*

Number of Pupils for whom tuition is paid? *6*

Number of White Pupils? *1* How many hours have you taught per day? *6*

Number always present? *2* How many days have you taught this month? *Bort the 17th ...*

Number always punctual? *2*

Number over 16 years of age? *1* { Give reasons for deficiency of time, (if any,) in teaching. }

Number in Alphabet? *2*

Number who spell, and read easy lessons? *2*

Number in advanced readers? *5*

Number in Geography? *4*

Number in Arithmetic? *6* *mental arith.*

Number in higher branches? *0*

Number in Writing? *0*

Number in Needle-work? *0*

Number free before the war? *1*

Have you a Sabbath-School? *No* How many Teachers? *0* How many Pupils? *0*

Have you an Industrial School? *No* How many Teachers? *0* How many Pupils? *0*

State the kind of work done? *Training*

☞ To the following questions give exact or approximate answers, prefixing to the latter the word "about."

1 Do you know of any Schools for Refugees or Freedmen not reported to the State Superintendent? How many?

2 Give (estimated) whole number of pupils in all such Schools? No. of Teachers, White, Colored.

3. Do you know of Sabbath Schools not reported to the State Superintendent? *Yes* How many? *1*

4. Give (estimated) whole number of pupils in all such Schools? No. of Teachers, White, Colored.

5. State the public sentiment towards Colored Schools,

6. How many pupils in your School are members of a Temperance Society? *1* Name of the Society? *B.O.G.S. or A*

Remarks. *The people are not able to pay the tuition, but they want to send their children to school.*

(Signed) *Sam. C. Windsor*

* A School Organization, either District, Town, City, County, or State.
† A pupil is not to be reckoned as enrolled until after five days' attendance.

22    23

Register of Marriages among Freedmen in ... Philadelphia, during year 1865

| Date 1865 | Name of Male | Place of Residence | Name of Female | Place of Residence | Age | Color | Color of Father |
|---|---|---|---|---|---|---|---|
| August 9 | Edward Tate | Clark Co. | Margaret Tate | Clark Co. | 25 | Dark | |
| " 12 | George Heard | " " | Lish Ann Shackleford | " " | 26 | do. | Dark |
| 6 | Miles Traswick | " " | Caroline Stuart | " " | 25 | " | " |
| Sept. 3 | Washington Gillet | " " | Harriet Townsend | " " | 61 | " | " |

## Marriage

While many slave couples formed lasting bonds during their enslavement, slave marriages had no legal foundation or protection. The abolishment of slavery granted not only citizenship but also the ability to have legally recognized marriages without fear of the loss of a spouse through sale. The Bureau helped facilitate and record marriages.

opposite page and below (detail):

**"Register of Marriages among Freedmen in Arkadelphia during year 1865"**

*National Archives, Records of the Bureau of Refugees, Freedmen, and Abandoned Lands*

On August 9, 1865, Edward Tate married Margaret Tate, who had been separated from her previous partner by sale, as had 52-year-old Rachel Cole, who married 80-year-old John Barter on September 10.

**Marriage Certificate for Peter Thompson and Maria Hall, January 28, 1867**

*National Archives, Records of the Bureau of Refugees, Freedmen, and Abandoned Lands*

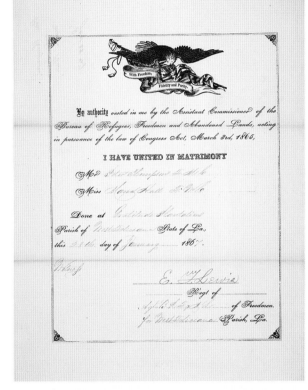

23

| | Separated by | No. of children by previous compan't. | Age | Color | No. of Father | No. of Mother | Lived with another man years. | No. of Children by previous Companion | Separated by | No. of children united | Name of Officiating Minister |
|---|---|---|---|---|---|---|---|---|---|---|---|
| rs | adultery | 3 | 28 | Black | | Light | 5 yrs | 2 | being sold | | W. W. Carmichael J. P. |
| " | " | 1 | 16 | Yellow | White | dark | — | — | — | | " " " |
| " | her consent | 1 | 25 | dark | — | — | — | — | — | | " " " |
| yrs | Death | 8 | 40½ | Copper | White | dark | 9 " | 4 | no cause | | " " " |

Arkadelphia, during year 1865

Female

**Memorandum of an Agreement to lease land to L. J. Coker from William G. Brounlory, May 15, 1865**

*National Archives, Records of the Bureau of Refugees, Freedmen, and Abandoned Lands*

# MEMORANDUM OF AN AGREEMENT

Made this *23* day of *March* 186*5*, between *Wm G.*
*Brounlory Spl* ———— Special Agent of the Treasury Department, duly appointed under the Acts of Congress respectively approved March 12, 1863, and July 2, 1864, for taking charge of captured and abandoned property, and leasing abandoned and confiscable lands, houses, and tenements in the *First Special* Agency, and *L. J. Coker* of *Knoxville* in the County of *Knox* and State of *Tennessee*

Witness, that in pursuance of said Acts, and of the Instructions of the Secretary of the Treasury, the said Agent, for and in behalf of the United States, agrees, upon the terms hereinafter contained, to lease to the said *L. J. Coker* from the *15* day of *May* 186*5*, from month to month, either party hereto being at liberty to terminate this lease at the end of any month from the date hereof, the following described premises: *A Small lot of land on Gay Stst. between the O. Keeth house & the widow Swans & belonging to Mrs. Hannah Swan*

And the said *L. J. Coker* hereby agrees to pay the said **Agent** *One* dollars per month, for each month from the date hereof, so long as he shall continue in possession of the said premises, and to pay the rent of each month in advance, and at the expiration of this lease as aforesaid to deliver possession of the said property to the said **Agent**, or his successor, in as good condition as the same is now in, loss by fire or other unavoidable injury excepted.

Signed, sealed and delivered }
in presence of }

*Jno. R. Henry*

*L. J. Coker*

*Wm. G. Brounlory*
*Spl. Spl. Agt. Try. Dept.*
*By Jno. R. Henry*

## Land

One of the major activities of the Bureau was the leasing of abandoned and confiscated property. Although their numbers were small, freedmen who had means were allowed to lease land ranging from ten to 100 acres. Their applications for land reveal the various resources applicants had and how they planned to use the land they were hoping to lease.

## Labor

The Bureau helped freedmen transition from slaves to paid laborers. Labor contracts capture some of the employment conditions freedmen faced immediately after emancipation.

**Agreement of Labor for Montgomery and seventeen others with Lipscomb, December 24, 1866**
*National Archives, Records of the Bureau of Refugees, Freedmen, and Abandoned Lands*

Federal records are a treasure chest of genealogical information, and there's a good chance that you or someone in your family is represented among the National Archives' holdings.

Each year, millions of people use records in the National Archives to search for their family roots. Census schedules, ship passenger arrival lists, citizenship papers, military pension files, land patents, and court records offer detailed evidence to flesh out family histories. In-depth family history research is time consuming. But with patience, you might unearth a wealth of documentation.

**Q.** My great-grandfather traveled abroad extensively. Is he in the Archives?

**A.** It's likely, depending on the dates. The National Archives has passport records from 1790 to 1949, including passport applications from 1795 to March 31, 1925.

Passport application records usually contain the applicant's name, signature, date and place of birth, marital status, date and place of naturalization (if foreign born), place of residence, and physical description. They also give the names or number of persons intending to travel and the date and destination of travel. Applications dating from December 1914 through March 1925 are accompanied by photographs of applicants.

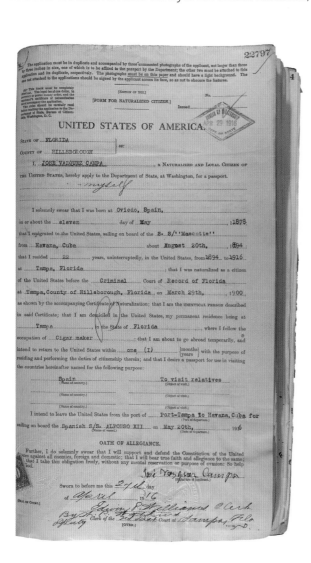

**Passport application for Jose Vazquez Campa, April 27, 1916**
*National Archives, General Records of the Department of State*

opposite page:
**United States Lines, "Leviathan at Southampton," poster, not dated**
*National Archives, Records of the U.S. Shipping Board (32-P-1)*

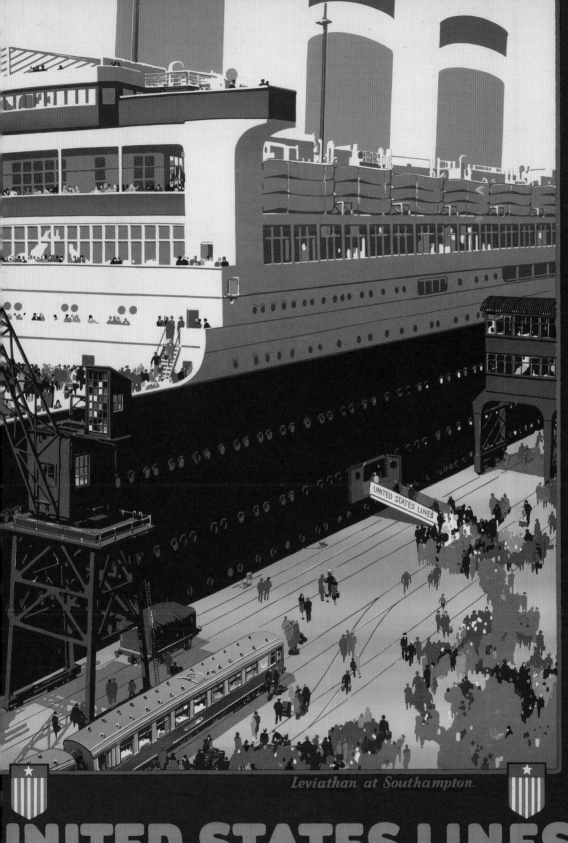

*Leviathan at Southampton.*

# UNITED STATES LINES
## *Europe – America*

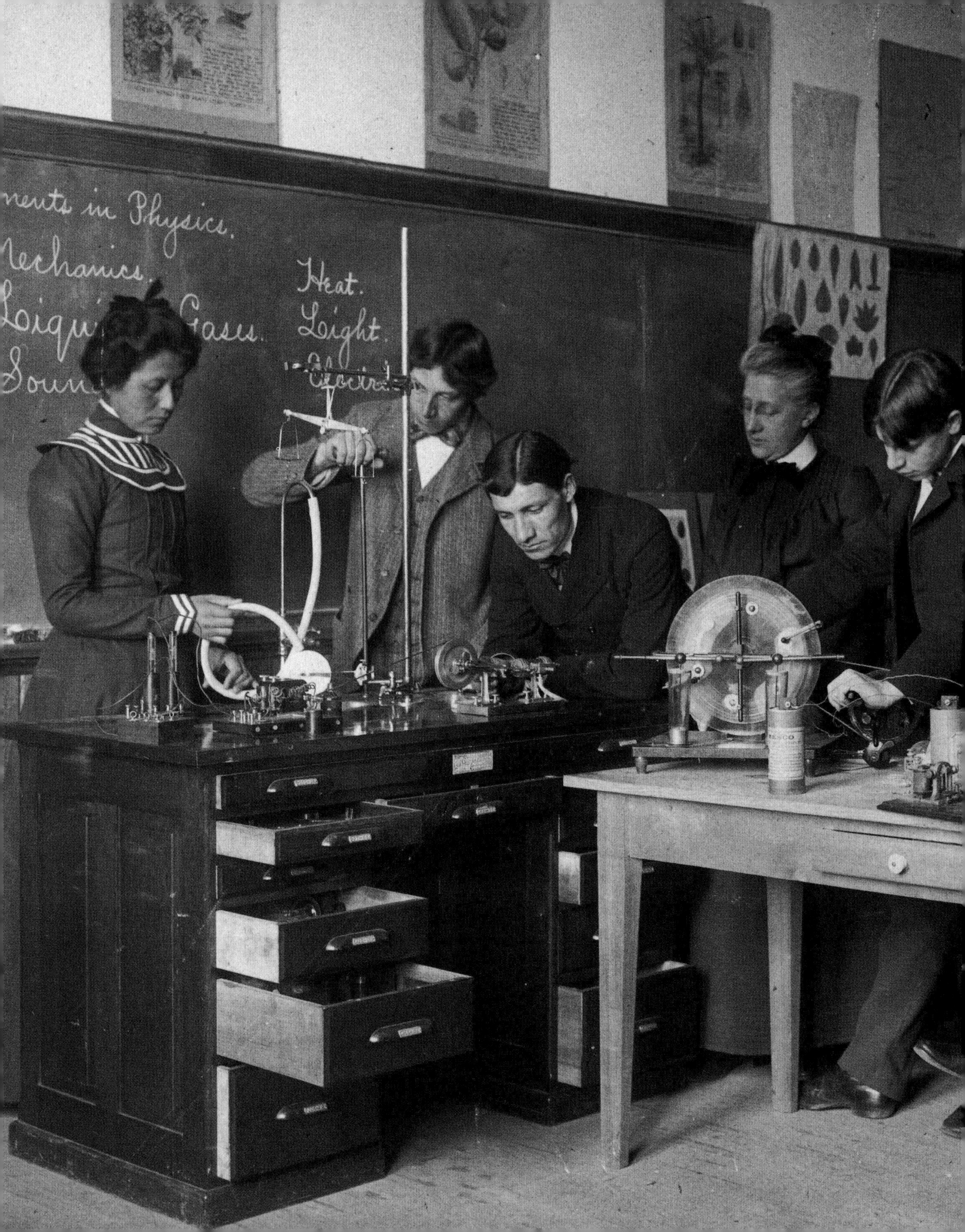
nents in Physics.
Mechanics.
Heat.
Light.

Q. One of my ancestors attended the Carlisle Indian Industrial School in Pennsylvania. Is he in the Archives?

A. Possibly. Because some schools for Native Americans were under the Federal Government's jurisdiction, the National Archives holds their administrative files.

Student records for these schools are part of the administrative files. School records include grade reports, disciplinary actions, newspaper clippings, photographs, and information such as addresses and names of relatives.

bottom right:
**Jim Thorpe, ca. 1910**
*National Archives, Records of the Bureau of Indian Affairs*

below:
**Student information card for Jim Thorpe, ca. 1904–13**
*National Archives, Records of the Bureau of Indian Affairs*

opposite page:
**Physics classroom at Carlisle Indian School, Pennsylvania, 1915**
*National Archives, Records of the Bureau of Indian Affairs (75-EXC-6D)*

**Q.** I was born in the United States in 1929. Am I in the Archives?

**A.** It's likely. The National Archives holds the 1930 census schedules listing 123 million Americans living in the United States at that time.

The National Archives also holds census schedules for every decennial census—those taken every ten years—since the first in 1790. Census schedules from 1790 to 1930 are available on microfilm in Washington, DC, and at regional archives facilities.

inset:
**"Community hospital, Hutchinson, Minnesota, 1924,"** 1924
*National Archives, Records of the Bureau of Agricultural Economics (83-ML-10309)*

**Detail from the 1930 census showing ward 19, block 2266, Milwaukee, Wisconsin, April 10, 1930**
*National Archives, Records of the Bureau of the Census*

People search the records of the National Archives for family records as a recreational activity or as a way to establish their rights. Every year an estimated 200,000 genealogical researchers use the voluminous records held at the Research Center in the National Archives Building in Washington, DC; the National Archives in College Park, Maryland; the military and civilian personnel records centers in St. Louis, Missouri; and regional archives facilities.

Searching for one individual in a sea of records requires time and patience. Fortunately for researchers, the most heavily used records—such as census records and ship passenger logs—are available on microfilm. And staff and volunteers are always on hand to help launch new genealogists.

## Proving Citizenship

Stories are passed down through generations, but family lore often needs verification. Proof of citizenship is necessary, for example, to receive Social Security payments. One record you may find at the National Archives to help prove a family member's citizenship is a ship's log of passengers arriving in America. Ship logs can prove the date of an individual's arrival in America as well as his or her age and occupation and intended place of residence. The arrival record may also include notations from immigration officials, which provide clues that an individual applied for citizenship. Census records also provide valuable information, such as where your ancestors lived and their occupations. But the key records for proving citizenship are the petitions for citizenship and oaths of allegiance.

**Young boy holding infant, 1924**
*National Archives, Gerald R. Ford Library (A-H0017[02])*

overleaf:
**Passenger arrival list in the Port of New York on the SS *Acropolis*, June 26, 1921**
*National Archives, Records of the Immigration and Naturalization Service*

# LIST OR MANIFEST OF ALIEN PASSENGERS FOR THE UNITE

ALL ALIENS arriving at a port of continental United States from a foreign port or a port of the insular possessions of the United States, and all aliens arriving at a port of said insular possessions from a foreign port, a port of continental U

This (white) sheet is for the listing

S. S. S.S. ACROPOLIS . Passengers sailing from CONSTANTINOPLE , MAY 26, 1921 , 19

| HEAD-TAX STATUS. | NAME IN FULL. Family name. | Given name. | Age. Yrs. | Mos. | Sex. | Married or single. | Calling or occupation. | Read. | Able to— Read what language | Write. | Nationality. (Country of which citizen or subject.) | Race or people. | Last permanent residence. Country. | City or town. | The name and complete address of nearest relative or friend in country whence alien came. | Final destination. State. | City or town |
|---|---|---|---|---|---|---|---|---|---|---|---|---|---|---|---|---|---|
| | Arakelian | Hripsime | 35 | | F | M | None | Yes | Armenian | Yes | Armenia | Armenian | Turkey | Cons/ple | BROTHER: Rupen Kahfedjian Koumkapou, Cons/ple Turkey | R.I. | Provedenc |
| UNDER 16 | " Son | Krikor | 10 | | M | S | None | Yes | do | Yes | do | do | do | do | do | do | do |
| UNDER 16 | " Daught. | Elisa | 8 | | F | S | None | Yes | do | Yes | do | do | do | do | do | do | do |
| | Tchidouni | Migran | 45 | | M | M | Busine ss.Comm | Yes | French | Yes | Persia | Armenian | Turkey | Cons/ple | UNCLE: Ohannes Agopian, Stamboul; Cons/ple Turkey | Calf. | Fresno |
| | " Wife | Almaste | 38 | | F | M | None | No | do | No | do | do | do | do | do | do | do |
| UNDER 16 | " Son | Karnik | 8 | | M | S | None | No | do | No | do | do | do | do | do | do | do |
| UNDER 16 | " Son | Kourken | 6 | | M | S | None | No | do | No | do | do | do | do | do | do | do |
| | Tachdjian | Sirarpi | 19 | | F | S | None | Yes | Armenian | Yes | Armenia | Armenian | Turkey | | COUSIN:Stephan Balayan Tophane, Cons/ple, Turkey | Mdine | Portland |
| | Pschayan | Mariam | 17 | | F | S | None | Yes | Roumenian | Yes | Roumenia | | | | FATHER: V. Passayian, Kadikey, Cons/ple, Turkey | ILL. | E.St.Louis |
| | Sirounien | Housakin | 25 | | M | M | Carpen ter | Yes | Armenian | Yes | | | | | FRIEND: Karakin Touripyan Scutari, Cons/ple Turkey | Maine | Portland |
| | " Wife | Zarouhi | 18 | | F | M | None | Yes | do | Yes | do | | | | do | do | do |
| | Tivanian | Krikor | 28 | | M | M | Laborer | Yes | do | Yes | do | | | | FRIEND: Melkon Kotsoyian Scutari, Cons/ple, Turkey | Maine | Portland |
| | " Wife | Nevarti | 24 | | F | M | None | Yes | do | Yes | do | | | | do | do | do |
| UNDER 16 | " Son | Kasbar | | 3 | M | S | None | | INFANT | | do | | | | do | do | do |
| | Tevalian | Rakel | 18 | | F | S | None | Yes | Armenia | Armenian | Turkey | Cons/ple | | | FRIEND: Horbannes Vartanian Scutari, Cons/ple, Turkey | Maine | Portland |
| | Amerikian | Mikael | 35 | | M | M | Carpen ter | Yes | do | Yes | Turkey | | | | FRIEND: Serkis Sourigian Kouran Oglou,Cons/ple Tkr | Maine | Portland |
| | " Wife | Nartache | 23 | | F | M | None | No | No | No | | | | | do | do | do |
| UNDER 16 | " Son | Vrege | | 2 | M | | INFANT | | | | | | | | do | do | do |
| | Amerikian | Araexia | 36 | | F | M | Homwrk | Yes | Armenian | Yes | | | | | | Maine | Portland |
| | Vartanian | Narkize | 27 | | F | M | None | Yes | do | Yes | Turkey | | | | RELATIVE: Dikran Danidian Galata, Cons/ple Turkey | Mich | Detroit |
| | Beklian | Ughaper | 45 | | F | M | None | Yes | do | Yes | Armenia | | | | COUSIN: Bikian Danielian Cons/ple, Turkey | ILL. | Waukegan |
| UNDER 16 | " Son | Manouk | 5 | | M | S | None | No | do | No | do | | | | do | do | do |
| | Garabedian | Eghia | 43 | | M | M | Carpen ter | Yes | Armenian | Yes | | | | | FRIEND: Tanielian Pershenbe Galata, Cons/ple Turkey | Mich | Detroit |
| | " Wife | Verkine | 35 | | F | M | None | Yes | do | Yes | | | | | do | do | do |
| | " Daught. | Vartanouiche | 16 | | F | S | None | Yes | do | Yes | | | | | do | do | do |
| UNDER 16 | " Daught. | Arpenik | 2 | | F | S | None | | INFANT | | | | | | do | do | do |
| | Beklian | Choghagat | 18 | | F | S | None | Yes | Armenia | Armenian | Turkey | Cons/ple | | | COUSIN: T.Tamehian Galata; Cons/ple Turkey | ILL. | Waukegan |
| | Bodikian | Arsen | 20 | | M | S | Cook | Yes | do | Yes | do | | | | FRIEND: Gabriel Hasarosian Galata; Cons/ple Turkey | Mich | Detroit |
| | Assadourian | Levon | 19 | | M | S | Farm Laborer | Yes | do | Yes | do | | do | do | BROTHER: Arshak Assadourian Stamboul; Cons/ple Turkey | Mich | Detroit |
| | Charkioglou | Constantin | 25 | | M | S | Carpen ter | Yes | Greek | Yes | Turkey | Greek | Turkey | Echanak | FATHER: Eustratios Charkioglou Echanak, Turkey | Pa. | Phila. |

* Permanent residence within the meaning of this manifest shall be actual or intended residence of one year or more.
† List of races will be found on the back of this sheet.

Total passengers . . . . 404
U. S. citizens . . . . . 15

...es, or a port of another insular possession, in whatsoever class they travel, MUST be fully listed and the master or commanding officer of each vessel carrying such passengers must upon arrival deliver lists thereof to the immigration officer.
ERAGE PASSENGERS ONLY

...rriving at Port of **NEW-YORK** , **JUNE 25, 1921** , _19_        247

| 15 | 16 | 17 | 18 | | 19 | 20 | 21 | 22 | 23 | 24 | 25 | 26 | 27 | 28 | 29 | 30 | 31 | | 32 | 33 | |
|---|---|---|---|---|---|---|---|---|---|---|---|---|---|---|---|---|---|---|---|---|---|
| Whether having a ticket to such final destination. | By whom was passage paid? | Whether in possession of $50, and if less, how much. | Whether ever before in the United States; and if so, when and where? | | Whether going to join a relative or friend; and if so, what relative or friend, and his name and complete address. | Purpose of coming to United States. | | Whether a polygamist. | Whether an anarchist. | | | Whether alien had been previously | Condition of health, mental and physical. | Deformed or crippled. Nature, length of time, and cause. | Height. | | Color of— | | Marks of identification. | Place of birth. | |
| | | | Yes or No. | If yes—Year or period of years. Where? | | | | | | | | | | | Feet. Inches. | Complexion. | Hair. | Eyes. | | Country. | City or town. |
| NO | Self | 50 | NO | — — | DAUGHTER: R.Setrak Krikorian   16 Bank St.Providence, R.I. | NO | Perman | Yes | NO | N N | NO | NO | NO | Good | NO | 5 1 | Dkr | Gry | Blue | None | Turkey | Angora |
| NO | -- | - | NO | — — | do   do   do | NO | do | Yes | NO | N N | NO | NO | NO | Good | NO | 4 1 | " | Brw | Blue | None | do | do |
| NO | -- | - | NO | — — | do   do   do | NO | do | Yes | NO | N N | NO | NO | NO | Good | NO | 4 | rdy | Brw | Brw | None | do | do |
| NO | Self | Yes | NO | — — | SISTERINLAW: H.K.Darbinian   President ST.Fresno, Calf. | NO | Perman | Yes | NO | N N | NO | NO | NO | Good | NO | 6 | Dkr | Blk | Brw | Small pox marks | Persia | Salenas |
| NO | -- | - | NO | — — | do   do   do | NO | do | Yes | NO | N N | NO | NO | NO | Good | NO | 5 3 | Dkr | Blk | Blk | None | do | do |
| NO | -- | - | NO | — — | do   do   do | NO | do | Yes | NO | N N | NO | NO | NO | Good | NO | 4 6 | " | Brw | Brw | None | do | Tiflis |
| NO | -- | - | NO | — — | do   do   do | NO | do | Yes | NO | N N | NO | NO | NO | Good | NO | 4 | " | " | " | None | do | do |
| NO | Self | 50 | NO | — — | HER FIANCE: Moovses Kaklegian   144Lancaster St.Portland,Maine | NO | do | Yes | NON | N | NO | N | NO | Good | NO | 5 2 | Dkr | Brw | Brw | None | Turkey | Kadikeny |
| NO | Her Fiance | 50 | NO | — — | HER FIANCE: Paravon Terzian   1438 Brady Ave.East St.Louis ILL. | NO | Perman | Yes | NO | N N | NO | NO | NO | Good | NO | 5 | Dkr | Brw | Brw | None | Turkey | Erzeroum |
| NO | Self | Yes | NO | — — | BROTHER: Aram Serunian,   190 Oxford St.Portland,Maine | NO | do | Yes | NO | N N | NO | NO | NO | Good | NO | 5 10 | Rdy | Brw | Gry | None | do | do |
| NO | Husband | - | NO | — — | do   do   do | NO | Perman | Yes | NO | N N | NO | NO | NO | Good | NO | 4 3 | Dkr | Brw | Brw | None | do | do |
| NO | Self | Yes | NO | — — | FATHER: Hairebet Tivanian,   166 Lane St.Portland, Maine | NO | do | Yes | NO | N N | NO | NO | NO | Good | NO | 5 5 | lgt | Brw | Blue | None | do | Erzeroum |
| NO | Husband | - | NO | — — | do   do   do | NO | Perman | Yes | NO | N N | NO | NO | NO | Good | NO | 5 1 | Dkr | Brw | Brw | None | do | Cons/ple |
| NO | -- | - | INFANT | — — | do   do   do | do | do | do | — | — — | — | — | — | Good | NO | — 3 | INFANT | | | None | do | do |
| NO | Brother | 50 | NO | — — | BROTHER: Givagos Tevanian   166 Lancaster St.Portland,Maine | NO | Perman | Yes | NO | N N | NO | NO | NO | Good | NO | 5 | Dkr | Blk | Brw | None | Turkey | Erzeroum |
| NO | Self | Yes | YES | 1911 Portlnd 1913 Maine | BROTHER: Amewart Amerikian   166 Lancaster ST.Portland Ma. | NO | do | Yes | NO | N N | NO | NO | NO | Good | NO | 5 10 | Rdy | Blk | Gry | None | do | do |
| NO | Husband | No | NO | — — | do   do   do | NO | do | Yes | NO | N N | NO | NO | NO | Good | NO | 5 7 | Dkr | Blk | Brw | None | do | do |
| NO | -- | - | - | — — | do   do   do | NO | do | Yes | NO | N N | NO | NO | NO | Good | NO | INFANT | | | | None | Turkey | Cons/ple |
| NO | Husband | 50 | NO | — — | HUSBAND: Amewart Amerikian,   166 Lancaster ST.Portland M | NO | Perman | Yes | NO | N N | NO | NO | NO | Good | NO | 5 | Dkr | Blk | Brw | None | " | Erzeroum |
| NO | Husband | 50 | NO | — — | HUSBAND: Avedi Vartanian   253 W.Fort St.Detroit,Mich | NO | Perman | Yes | NO | N N | NO | NO | NO | Good | NO | 5 4 | Dkr | brw | brw | None | Armenia | Ersindjan |
| NO | Self | 40 | NO | — — | NEPHEW: K.Bechlian 715 Sutica   St.Waukegan, Ill. | NO | Perman | Yes | NO | N N | NO | NO | NO | Good | NO | 4 10 | mx | Blk | Blk | None | " | do |
| NO | -- | - | NO | — — | do   do   do | NO | do | Yes | NO | N N | NO | NO | NO | Good | NO | 5 6 | Dkr | Brw | Brw | None | " | do |
| NO | Self | Yes | NO | — — | BROTHER: H.Garabetian 253   Fort St W.Detroit, Mich | NO | do | Yes | NO | N N | NO | NO | NO | Good | NO | 5 8 | " | Blk | Blk | Ball Head | Turkey | Erzenga |
| NO | -- | - | NO | — — | do   do   do | NO | Perman | Yes | NO | N N | NO | NO | NO | Good | NO | 5 2 | " | " | " | None | do | do |
| NO | -- | - | NO | — — | do   do   do | NO | do | Yes | NO | N N | NO | NO | NO | Good | NO | 5 1 | Dkr | " | " | Scar a Tatto on chin | do | do |
| NO | -- | - | - | — — | do   do   do | NO | do | do | — | — — | — | — | — | Measles Good | — | INFANT | | — | — | None | do | do |
| NO | Brother | 50 | NO | — — | BROTHER:K.Beklian, 715   Sutica St.Waukegan, Ill. | NO | Perm. | Yes | NO | N N | NO | NO | NO | Good | NO | 4 9 | Dkr | Brw | Brw | None | Turkey | Ersingian |
| NO | Self | 30 | NO | — — | COUSIN: Hovames Bodigian   Quebec, Mich | NO | do | Yes | NO | N N | NO | NO | NO | Good | NO | 5 5 | Dkr | Blk | Brw | None | Armenia | Ersintgan |
| NO | Self | 50 | NO | — — | STEPFATHER:Kosrof Houanessian   1536 Kenall Ave.Detroit, Mich | NO | Perman | Yes | NO | N N | NO | NO | NO | Good | NO | 5 | Dkr | Blk | Brw | Small pox marks, face | Turkey | Van |
| NO | Self | 50 | NO | — — | BROTHER: Gerasimos Efstigtain   2824 Richmond St.Phila.Pa. | NO | Perman | Yes | NO | N N | NO | NO | NO | Good | NO | 5 7 | " | Brw | Brw | None | do | Dardanell |

**Petition for citizenship for Mikael Amerikian, July 7, 1931**

*National Archives–Northeast Region (Boston), Records of the District Courts of the United States*

If one document alone cannot provide the proof you seek to prove your citizenship or that of a family member, a collection of documents that tell a story may. Dates, place-names, and any other known details help an archivist find your ancestors in the records. Keep in mind that new immigrants to this country often eventually change the spelling of their last names, so that a family name may be spelled differently in a later generation.

ORIGINAL

# UNITED STATES OF AMERICA
## PETITION FOR CITIZENSHIP

No. 5046

To the Honorable the __U.S. District__ Court of __Maine__ at __Portland__

The petition of __MIKAEL AMERIKIAN__ hereby filed, respectfully shows:

(1) My place of residence is __69 Oxford street, Portland__ (2) My occupation is __Grocer__

(3) I was born in __Ezroom, Turkey__ on __April, 1885__ My race is __Armenian__

(4) I declared my intention to become a citizen of the United States on __April 10, 1929__ in the __U.S. District__ Court of __Maine District__, at __Portland, Maine__

(5) I am __married__. The name of my wife or husband is __Nortivee (Torosian) Amerikian__ we were married on __Nov. 19, 1918__ at __Armenia__; She was born at __Exroom, Turkey__ on __1898__ entered the United States at __New York,__ on __June 26, 1921__ for permanent residence therein, and now resides at __Portland, Maine__ I have __6__ children, and the name, date, and place of birth, and place of residence of each of said children are as follows: __Verag, born 3/10/21, at Constantiple; Vergina, born 4/20/22; Vasken, born 9/25/24; Mary, born 1/12/26; Doloris, born 11/6/29; Nazarett, born 10/28/27; all but first born in Portland, Me. and all reside in Portland, Me.__

(6) My last foreign residence was __Constantinople, Turkey__ I emigrated to the United States of America from __Constantinople, Turkey__ My lawful entry for permanent residence in the United States was at __New York, N.Y.__ under the name of __Mikael Amerikian__ on __June 26, 1921__, on the vessel __SS Acropolis__ as shown by the certificate of my arrival attached hereto.

(7) I am not a disbeliever in or opposed to organized government or a member of or affiliated with any organization or body of persons teaching disbelief in or opposed to organized government. I am not a polygamist nor a believer in the practice of polygamy. I am attached to the principles of the Constitution of the United States and well disposed to the good order and happiness of the United States. It is my intention to become a citizen of the United States and to renounce absolutely and forever all allegiance and fidelity to any foreign prince, potentate, state, or sovereignty, and particularly to __The Republic of Turkey__ of whom (which) at this time I am a subject (or citizen), and it is my intention to reside permanently in the United States. (8) I am able to speak the English language. (9) I have resided continuously in the United States of America for the term of five years at least immediately preceding the date of this petition, to wit, since __June 26, 1921__ and in the County of __Cumberland__ this State, continuously next preceding the date of this petition, since __June 26, 1921__, being a residence within said county of at least six months next preceding the date of this petition.

(10) I have __not__ heretofore made petition for citizenship: Number _____, on _____ at _____ and such petition was denied by that Court for the following reasons and causes, to wit: _____ and the cause of such denial has since been cured or removed.

Attached hereto and made a part of this, my petition for citizenship, are my declaration of intention to become a citizen of the United States, certificate from the Department of Labor of my said arrival, and the affidavits of the two verifying witnesses required by law.

Wherefore, I, your petitioner, pray that I may be admitted a citizen of the United States of America, and that my name be changed to _____

I, your aforesaid petitioner being duly sworn, depose and say that I have {read/heard read} this petition and know the contents thereof; that the same is true of my own knowledge except as to matters therein stated to be alleged upon information and belief, and that as to those matters I believe it to be true; and that this petition is signed by me with my full, true name.

*mikeil amerikian*
(Complete and true signature of petitioner)

## AFFIDAVITS OF WITNESSES

__Nathan Asdoorian__ occupation __Barber__ residing at __3 Oxford Place, Portland, Maine__ and __Sam Eloian__, occupation __Berber__ residing at __4 Oxford Place, Portland, Me.__ each being severally, duly, and respectively sworn, deposes and says that he is a citizen of the United States of America; that he has personally known and has been acquainted in the United States with __Mikael Amerikian__, the petitioner above mentioned, since __July, 1921__ and that to his personal knowledge the petitioner has resided in the United States continuously preceding the date of filing this petition, of which this affidavit is a part, to wit, since the date last mentioned, and at __Portland__, in the County of __Cumberland__ this State, in which the above-entitled petition is made, continuously since __July, 1921__, and that he has personal knowledge that the petitioner is and during all such periods has been a person of good moral character, attached to the principles of the Constitution of the United States, and well disposed to the good order and happiness of the United States, and that in his opinion the petitioner is in every way qualified to be admitted a citizen of the United States

*Nathan Asdourian*
(Signature of witness)

*Sam Eloian*
(Signature of witness)

Subscribed and sworn to before me by the above-named petitioner and witnesses in the office of the Clerk of said Court at __Portland__ this __7th__ day of __July__, Anno Domini 19__31__ I hereby certify that certificate of arrival No. __1-64728__ from the Department of Labor, showing the lawful entry for permanent residence of the petitioner above named, together with declaration of intention No. __8830 58384__ of such petitioner, has been by me filed with, attached to, and made a part of this petition on this date.

John F. Knowlton
Clerk.
By *Mary E. Bulger*
Deputy Clerk.

(SEAL.)

No. 239063

Form 2204-L-A U. S. DEPARTMENT OF LABOR NATURALIZATION SERVICE 14—3618

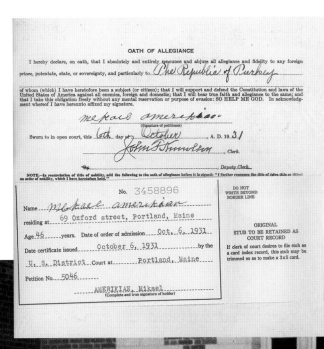

Oath of allegiance of Mikael Amerikian, October 6, 1931

*National Archives–Northeast Region (Boston), Records of the District Courts of the United States*

below:

**Immigrants standing outside of building with young girl in front covering her eyes, 1917–19**

*National Archives, Records of the Public Health Service (90-G-125-9)*

District of Vermont

The President of the United States
To the Marshal of the District of Vermont

Whereas Mathew Lyon of Fairhaven in the County
of Rutland in the District of Vermont before the Circuit Court
of the United States begun & held at Rutland within and
for the said district on the Third day of October in the year
of our Lord One thousand seven hundred and ninety eight
and of the Independence of the said United States the twenty third
convicted of writing, Printing, uttering & publishing certain
false scandalous & seditious Libels, and of aiding abetting
and assisting therein – contrary to the form force & effect of
the Statute entitled "an Act in addition to an Act entitled
"an Act for the punishment of certain crimes against the
United States – and sentenced to imprisonment for the
term of four Calender Months, to pay a fine of one
thousand Dollars to the United States and the costs of this
Prosecution taxed at Sixty Dollars & Ninety six cents –
as appears of record whereof Execution remains to be done –

Therefore by the Authority of the United States you are
hereby commanded to imprison him the said Mathew
Lyon in either of the Goals of the United States within and
for the District of Vermont for the Term of four callender m
from the date hereof – and on his the said Mathew Lyon
neglect or refusal to pay said fine and cost you are to
and detain him the said Mathew in imprisonme
afsd. until he pay the said fine with fifty sixty for the
of commitment together with your fees, and cost and
discharged according to Law – and cost you are to
And of this writ with your doings herein make
according to Law at our said Court on the first day
Witness the Honorable Oliver Ellsworth
of the Supreme Court of the United Sta
on aforesaid the ninth day of October at ea
thousand seven hundred
tendence of the said Unit

Cephas

# 3.

# FORM A MORE PERFECT UNION
## RECORDS OF LAWS AND JUSTICE

The National Archives holds the records that show the evolution of America's democracy. Both milestone documents and everyday records tell the story of the triumphs and struggles of the United States to become truly "one nation, with liberty and justice for all." The National Archives does not merely hold interesting antiquities; it holds the real evidence of public events—records used in the courtroom, the negotiation room, and the halls of Government to preserve rights, pursue justice, and hold governments accountable. Documents in this section show the interaction between citizens and government. It is a look behind the scenes at the records people use to establish their rights.

**Warrant for imprisonment of Mathew [sic] Lyon, October 9, 1798**
*National Archives–Northeast Region (Boston), Records of the District Courts of the United States*

Seven years after the Bill of Rights was ratified, guaranteeing freedom of speech, Congress passed the Sedition Act of 1798, prohibiting criticism of the Government. That same year, Congressman Matthew Lyon was convicted for criticizing President John Adams in a newspaper article. This document charged the U.S. Marshal for the District of Vermont to jail Lyon for four months and fine him $1,060.96. The act was allowed to expire two years later.

# CONSTITUTIONAL AMENDMENTS

Constitutional amendments, advised James Madison, should be reserved "for certain great and extraordinary occasions." Since 1789, more than 5,000 bills proposing amendments to the Constitution have been introduced in Congress. Only twenty-seven amendments have been ratified. To become part of the Constitution, an amendment must be approved by either a two-thirds vote of Congress or a national convention, then ratified by three-fourths of the state legislatures or conventions.

The first ten amendments, known as the Bill of Rights, enumerated the limits of Government power on individual liberties. Later amendments marked the end of the Civil War and slavery and broadened voting rights. One amendment—prohibiting the manufacture, sale, or transportation of alcoholic beverages—was ratified and then repealed.

top right:
**Petition from the citizens of Salem, Massachusetts, in favor of woman suffrage, ca. 1879**
*National Archives, Records of the U.S. Senate*

opposite page:
**A suffrage parade in New York City, 1912**
*National Archives, Records of the Office of War Information (208-PR-14M-1)*

bottom right:
**Memorial from Alice Wadsworth of the National Association Opposed to Woman Suffrage addressed to Representative Charles E. Fuller, December 11, 1917**
*National Archives, Records of the U.S. House of Representatives*

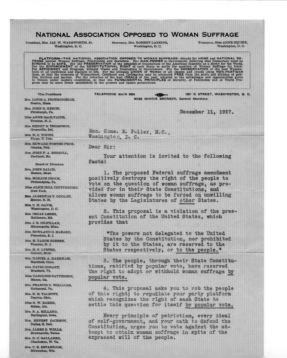

## Woman Suffrage and the 19th Amendment

For more than seventy years, beginning in the mid-1800s, champions of voting rights for women used a wide variety of strategies to achieve their goal. Some tried to pass suffrage acts in the states. Others challenged male-only voting laws in the courts. Suffragists sent petitions. They marched in parades, held vigils, and even went on hunger strikes. Opponents heckled, jailed, and sometimes physically abused them.

The first woman suffrage amendment was introduced in Congress in 1878. By 1916, almost all the major suffrage organizations had united behind the goal of a constitutional amendment granting women the right to vote. The House of Representatives and Senate passed the amendment that summer. On August 18, 1920, Tennessee became the thirty-sixth state to ratify the amendment. Eight days later, Secretary of State Bainbridge Colby certified the ratification.

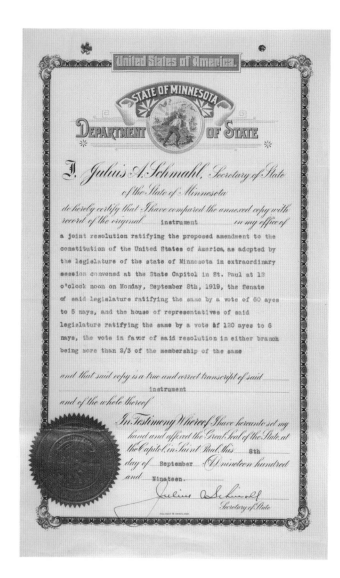

Ratification document for the
19th amendment from the State
of Minnesota, September 8, 1919
*National Archives, Records of the
U.S. House of Representatives*

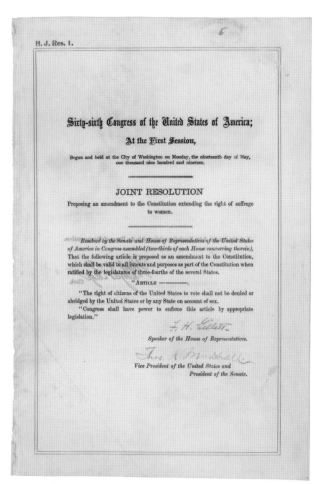

House Joint Resolution 1
proposing the 19th amendment to the
states, passed June 4, 1919
*National Archives, General Records of
the U.S. Government*

Whenever the President appears in public, the event provides an invaluable record of public policy . . . and also sheds light on the President's personality.

Whether they are formal addresses to the nation, regularly scheduled press conferences, televised town meetings, or photos taken with ordinary people, public events encourage an informed citizenry. The records of these events sometimes contain revealing moments of Presidential anger, frustration, and humor.

Within the holdings of the National Archives are thousands of hours of film, video, and sound recordings documenting the public promises and statements of Presidents.

"The differences among us are part of our strength, and the fact that we bring those differences to the surface, and get embarrassed by them sometimes, that means that we are facing them frankly.

We've never made progress in this country in the last 204 years by weakness or cowardice or by avoiding an issue just because it was difficult. And when we face the energy problem and when we try to do something about high interest rates and we try to do something about inflation or unemployment or trade, that's not a sign of weakness; it's a sign of strength. "

Jimmy Carter

Jimmy Carter is one of many Presidents presented in the audiovisual unit *White House: Public Platform.*

Even the behind-the-scenes moments of a President's administration eventually find their way into the National Archives.

Perhaps no other world leader is held more accountable than the President of the United States. As part of its mission, the National Archives assures access to the official actions of Presidents since Herbert Hoover. The process of documenting a President's administration includes compiling and preserving closed-door conversations, hastily scribbled notes, and unreleased letters and memos.

Researchers at the National Archives and its Presidential libraries can take advantage of the opportunity to read, watch, and listen to a variety of textual documents, motion pictures, and sound recordings that tell the inside story of the Presidency.

## Recordings from the Oval Office

Between 1940 and 1974, six Presidents used hidden microphones and audiotaping equipment to record White House meetings and telephone conversations. Although the secret recordings were never intended for public use, they are now an invaluable historical resource.

Nearly 2,400 hours of Oval Office discussions and telephone conversations from the Roosevelt, Truman, Eisenhower, Kennedy, Johnson, and Nixon administrations are available for research and purchase. The recordings were intended to be confidential. They represent the unguarded comments of the President of the United States, his most trusted advisors, and other public figures.

**Rose Mary Woods's White House tape recorder, ca. 1973**
*National Archives, Records of the District Courts of the United States*

Claiming executive privilege, President Richard Nixon offered Watergate investigators transcriptions of his taped conversations about the 1972 burglary of the Democratic Party headquarters instead of the actual tapes. Rose Mary Woods, secretary to the President, used this machine to transcribe one of the tapes. When she was finished, 18½ minutes of a conversation between the President and Chief of Staff H. R. Haldeman, probably related to the break-in, were found to be missing.

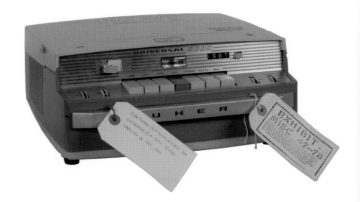

## President Reagan Is Shot

On March 30, 1981, only nine weeks after President Ronald Reagan took office, he was shot by John Hinckley, Jr. Vice President George Bush scribbled his feelings about the "enormity" of the event on a notepad while onboard a Presidential aircraft. Reagan, Press Secretary James Brady, Secret Service Agent Timothy McCarthy, and policeman Thomas Delahanty all survived the shooting.

right:
**Flight document with notes by Vice President Bush after President Reagan was shot, March 30, 1981**
*National Archives, George Bush Library*

below:
**President Ronald Reagan at the Washington Hilton Hotel, Washington, DC, just before he was shot**
*National Archives, Ronald Reagan Library (C1426-16)*

## The Johnson Treatment

On November 29, 1963, President Lyndon Baines Johnson recorded nineteen conversations in which he recruited people to serve on the President's Commission on the Assassination of President Kennedy, or the Warren Commission, which he was forming to investigate John F. Kennedy's assassination. Some, including Johnson's friend and mentor Senator Richard Russell, were reluctant to join. The Senator tried several tacks to refuse service on the commission, but President Johnson's persuasive style— which came to be known as the "Johnson Treatment"— was finally wearing him down. Senator Russell finally agreed to serve on the Warren Commission, which issued its report to the President on September 24, 1964.

**President Lyndon B. Johnson and Senator Richard Russell in the Oval Office, by Yoichi R. Okamoto, December 7, 1963**
*National Archives, Lyndon Baines Johnson Library (W-98-30)*

RUSSELL: Well now, Mr. President, I know I don't have to tell you of my devotion to you, but I just can't serve on that commission. I'm highly honored that you'd think about me in connection with it, but I couldn't serve there with Chief Justice Warren. I don't like that man. I don't have any confidence in him at all.

LBJ: Dick, . . . the reason I've asked Warren is because he is the chief justice of this country and we've got to have the highest judicial people we can have. The reason I ask you is because you have that same kind of temperament and you can do anything for your country and don't go giving me that kind of stuff about you can't serve with anybody. You can do anything.

RUSSELL:  I can't do it. I haven't got the time.
LBJ:  All right, we'll just make the time.
RUSSELL:  You're taking advantage of me but of course. . . .
LBJ:  . . . I'm going to be taking advantage of you a good deal, but you're going to serve your country and do what's right. . . . Why do you think I've done wrong now by appointing you on a commission?
RUSSELL:  Well, I just don't like Warren.
LBJ:  Well, of course you don't like Warren, but you'll like him before it is over with.
RUSSELL:  I haven't got any confidence in him.
LBJ:  Well, you can give him some confidence. . . .
RUSSELL:  Well, I'm not going to say anything more, Mr. President. I'm at your command.

Throughout American history, debates among members of Congress have helped shape the decisions that followed. Congressional debates are significant not only for the issues they raise but also for their fiery oratory, compelling arguments, and memorable speakers. Senators and representatives must make many difficult choices about matters as critical as going to war, raising or lowering taxes, and approving or voting down a constitutional amendment. Congressional deliberations provide an opportunity for members to explore and weigh the choices and to decide how, in the end, to cast their votes.

## War with Mexico

In early May 1846, sixteen U.S. soldiers died in battle with Mexican forces. On May 11, President James K. Polk asked Congress for a declaration of war. The Mexican Government did not recognize American sovereignty over Texas and felt free to send its troops into its own territory. President Polk believed that a state of war already existed and asked Congress to provide the means to wage it—in this case a "large body of volunteers." Later that month the House of Representatives debated H.R. 145, President Polk's request for acknowledgment of and provisions for the existing war with Mexico.

**"Map of Texas and the Countries Adjacent," 1844**
*National Archives, Records of the Office of the Chief of Engineers*

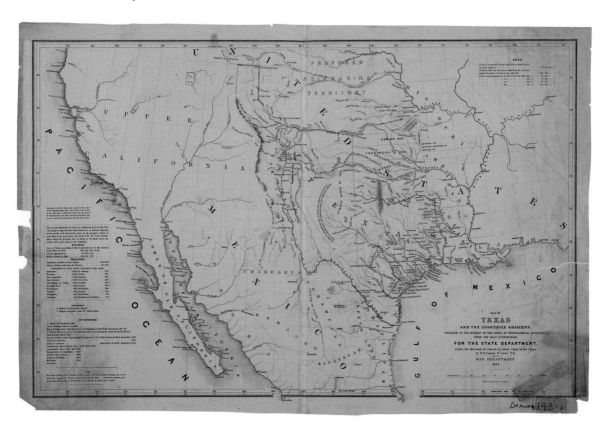

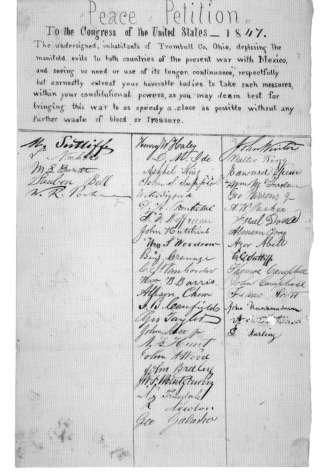

**"Peace Petition" to Congress from the inhabitants of Trumbull County, Ohio, 1847**
*National Archives, Records of the U.S. House of Representatives*

A year after the Mexican War began, debate over the war continued. Citizens of Trumbull County, Ohio, wrote to Congress and asked them to end the war.

## House of Representatives Debate on the Declaration of War with Mexico, 1846

Rep. I. E. Holmes, In Opposition
*We know nothing more that that the two armies have come into collision within the disputed territory, and I deny that war is absolutely, necessarily, the result of it. Suppose the Mexican Congress should not recognise the conduct of their general, and condemn it, and send here a remonstrance, or rather an apology—is it war? The invasion of any set of men in any capacity is not war. I remember—there are men on this floor who remember—all know that our frigate, the* Chesapeake, *was captured in 1807 by the frigate* Leopard. *Was that absolutely war? Will any man say that it created war?*

Rep. Brinkerhoff, In Favor
*Now; a state of war exists; hostilities have been commenced by the Mexican forces; the blood of American soldiers has been shed; guns have been fired; warlike operations are progressing. For myself I hold it to be no part of my duty to inquire how this war originated, nor wherefore; whether it was the fault of any one here, or of any one connected with this Government. It is enough for me, as a man professing an ordinary share of patriotism and representing a patriotic constituency, to know that it exists; and from this state of things, to arrive at the conclusion (necessarily, it seems to me) that our only course is to conquer peace by a vigorous prosecution of the war just commenced.*

## HOW WOULD YOU VOTE?

After the debate over the declaration of war with Mexico, the House of Representatives voted to declare war. The final vote was 173 yeas, 14 nays.

# COURTING FREEDOM

The evolution of civil rights in the United States is documented in Federal records preserved by the National Archives. More than 200 years after it was written, the U.S. Constitution remains the foundation of American law. The Constitution and its amendments constitute the yardstick against which all U.S. laws are measured. Interpretations of civil liberties have evolved and changed, however, as the events of American history have tested them.

The testing has often taken place in the Federal courts. The records of the judicial branch, held by the National Archives, highlight many crucial moments in the American experience—including evidence and judgments relating to the struggle for civil rights.

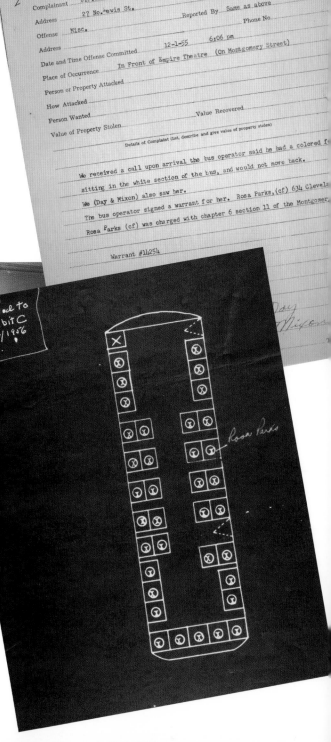

**County clerk swearing in a trial jury, ca. 1947**
*National Archives, Records of the U.S. Information Agency*
*(306-PS-176-S-51-141)*

POLICE DEPARTMENT
CITY OF MONTGOMERY

Misc.

Date 12-1-55 19

Complainant    J.F. Blake   (wm)                      Phone No.

Address        27 No. Lewis St.

Offense    Misc.                    Reported By   Same as above

Address                                            Phone No.

Date and Time Offense Committed      12-1-55      6:06 pm

Place of Occurrence    In Front of Empire Theatre  (On Montgomery Street)

Person or Property Attacked

How Attacked

Person Wanted                         Value Recovered

Value of Property Stolen

Details of Complaint (list, describe and give value of property stolen)

We received a call upon arrival the bus operator said he had a colored f
sitting in the white section of the bus, and would not move back.
We (Day & Mixon) also saw her.
The bus operator signed a warrant for her.  Rosa Parks, (cf) 634 Clevela
Rosa Parks (cf) was charged with chapter 6 section 11 of the Montgomer

Warrant #14254

EXHIBIT "A"
Attached to
Exhibit C
2/22/1956
WNR.

Rosa Parks

## The Rosa Parks Story

In 1955 a 42-year-old seamstress touched off a 381-day boycott of the Montgomery, Alabama, bus system when she was arrested for failing to yield her seat to a white man. A few days later, she was fined $10 plus $4 for court costs. A 26-year-old little-known minister, Martin Luther King, Jr., emerged as the leader of the Montgomery bus boycott.

This diagram showing where Rosa Parks was sitting when she refused to give up her seat to a white passenger was an exhibit in the *Browder* v. *Gayle* court case, which challenged Montgomery and Alabama laws requiring segregated seating on buses. On June 5, 1956, a Federal three-judge panel ruled that such laws violated the 14th Amendment. Later that year, the U.S. Supreme Court upheld the decision.

opposite page (top):

**Arrest report of Rosa Parks, December 1, 1955**

*National Archives–Southeast Region (Atlanta), Records of the District Courts of the United States*

opposite page (bottom):

**Diagram of bus showing where Rosa Parks was seated, December 1, 1955**

*National Archives–Southeast Region (Atlanta), Records of the District Courts of the United States*

## The Right to Representation

When Clarence Earl Gideon was accused of breaking and entering in Florida, he requested—but was denied—legal representation. Gideon was found guilty. On January 5, 1962, he submitted this petition to overturn the conviction to the U.S. Supreme Court. It ruled that the 14th Amendment required the "assistance of counsel as a fundamental right essential to a fair trial" and returned Gideon's case to the Florida court.

right:

**Petition of Clarence Earl Gideon, October Term, April 19, 1962**

*National Archives, Records of the Supreme Court of the United States*

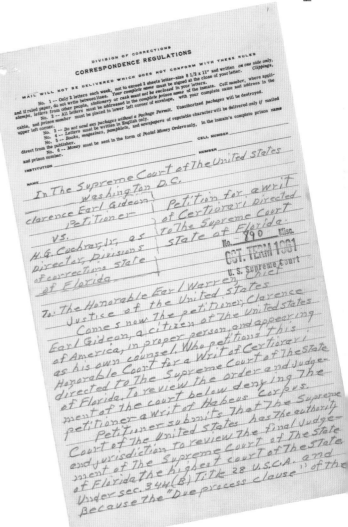

The Federal Government has launched probes into disasters, assassinations, civil unrest, unexplained phenomena, and puzzling social changes. Federal investigations shed light on what happened, who was accountable, and how to prevent similar events. They provide answers as well as evidence for controversies that last long after the actual events—sometimes after the Government's investigation has ended. Federal investigations are ways individuals can hold their government accountable and prove their entitlements as citizens.

The National Archives holds much of this investigatory information within the records of Federal commissions, boards, and committees. Other evidence comes to the Archives from Presidential or congressional investigations.

### Presidential Assassinations

Documents and evidence from investigations by the U.S. Army and the Warren Commission into the assassinations of Presidents Abraham Lincoln and John F. Kennedy, respectively, reside in the National Archives.

top right:
**John Wilkes Booth and fellow conspirators, not dated**
*National Archives, Records of the Office of the Chief Signal Officer (111-BA-92)*

A composite of photographs includes M. O'Laughlin with Booth and others who were proved to be fellow conspirators.

right:
**Telegram from John Wilkes Booth to M. O'Laughlin, March 19, 1864**
*National Archives, Records of the Office of the Judge Advocate General (Army)*

A telegram sent on March 19, 1864, from John Wilkes Booth to M. O'Laughlin, Esq., documents an important communication with Booth's friend from Baltimore, Maryland, a former Confederate soldier who worked in the produce and feed business.

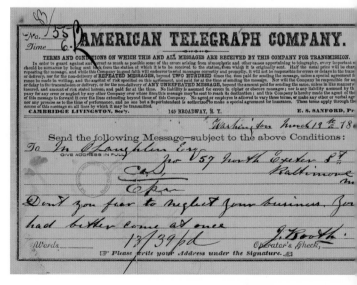

**The Zapruder Camera**

*National Archives, Records of the President's Commission on the Assassination of President Kennedy*

On November 22, 1963, when President John F. Kennedy made a visit to Dallas, Texas, Abraham Zapruder planned to attend the Presidential procession. That morning, Zapruder's secretary convinced him to return home for his movie camera, an 8mm Bell and Howell Zoomatic, to record the Presidential visit. Around noon, Zapruder left his office with the camera and went to nearby Dealey Plaza. At 12:30 P.M., he filmed the Kennedy motorcade just before, during, and immediately after the shooting. The twenty-six seconds of footage shot on this camera constitute the only complete film record of the assassination of President Kennedy.

**President and Mrs. Kennedy arrive at Love Field, Dallas, Texas, by Cecil Stoughton, November 22, 1963**

*National Archives, John F. Kennedy Library (ST-C420-13-63)*

**Lyndon B. Johnson takes the oath of office as President of the United States, after the assassination of President John F. Kennedy, by Cecil Stoughton, November 22, 1963**

*National Archives, Lyndon Baines Johnson Library*

# SAUCERS OVER WASHINGTON, D.C.

HARRY G. BARNES, SENIOR AIR ROUTE TRAFFIC CONTROLLER FOR THE CIVIL AERONAUTICS ADMINISTRATION, WAS IN CHARGE OF THE NATIONAL AIRPORT, WASHINGTON, D.C., A.R.T. CONTROL CENTER ON THE NIGHT OF JULY 19, 1952. "BRIEFY," HE STATES IN A NEWSPAPER ARTICLE, "...OUR JOB IS TO CONSTANTLY MONITOR THE SKIES AROUND THE NATION'S CAPITOL WITH THE ELECTRONIC EYE OF RADAR..." SHORTLY AFTER MIDNIGHT ON THAT DATE, SEVEN PIPS APPEARED SUDDENLY ON THE CONTROL CENTER'S SCOPE. ED NUGENT, JIM COPELAND, AND JIM RITCHEY, ALL EXPERIENCED RADAR CONTROLLERS, CHECKED THE OBSERVATIONS. THE AIRPORT CONTROL TOWER RADAR OPERATOR VERIFIED THE SAME SIGHTING. *THEY WERE OVER "THE RESTRICTED AREAS OF WASHINGTON,* INCLUDING THE *WHITE HOUSE* AND THE *CAPITOL..."*

CAPTAIN C.S. PIERMAN, A CAPITOL AIRLINES PILOT OF 17 YEARS FLYING EXPERIENCE, SHORTLY AFTER TAKING OFF, WAS ASKED TO CHECK THESE MYSTERIOUS OBJECTS. HE RADIOED BACK...

*THERE'S ONE... AND THERE IT GOES!*

PIERMAN DESCRIBED IT AS A BRIGHT LIGHT MOVING FASTER, AT TIMES, THAN A SHOOTING STAR...

BARNES STATES: "DURING THE NEXT 14 MINUTES, HE (PIERMAN) REPORTED THAT HE SAW SIX SUCH LIGHTS... *EACH SIGHTING COINCIDED WITH A PIP WE COULD SEE NEAR HIS PLANE.* WHEN *HE* REPORTED THAT THE LIGHT *STREAKED OFF AT HIGH SPEED,* IT *DISAPPEARED* FROM *OUR SCOPE..."*

THAT MEANS IT ZOOMED OUT OF OUR BEAM *BETWEEN SWEEPS!* IT *ACCELERATED* FROM *130* MILES PER HOUR TO ALMOST *500* IN LESS THAN *4 SECONDS...*

25

Two pages from the comic book "Saucers over Washington, D.C.," ca. 1952
*National Archives, Records of Headquarters U.S. Air Force (Air Staff)*

On July 19, 1952, air traffic controllers at Washington National Airport spotted several radar "blips" over Washington, DC. In addition, an airline pilot reported a fast-moving bright light. This comic book sensationalizing the sightings found its way into the Project Blue Book files.

## Project Blue Book: Unidentified Flying Objects

For more than twenty years, the Air Force, which was charged with the air defense of the United States, tracked sightings of unidentified flying objects (UFOs). Some believed the objects to be extraterrestrial spaceships. Project Blue Book was the code name for the most well known of the U.S. Air Force's investigations into UFOs.

## World War II War Crimes Tribunal: Nuremberg

During the twelve years of the Third Reich—between 1933 and 1945—the Jews of Nazi-controlled Europe were subjected to loss of property, exile, and near extermination. While the plans for the "final solution" were secret, organizing the actions was complex and generated much paperwork. A large number of these records were captured by the Allies and used as evidence in postwar trials held in Nuremberg, Germany.

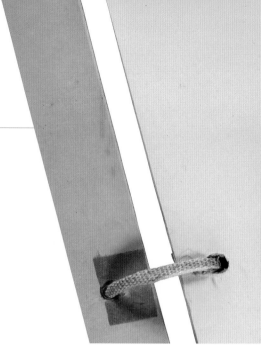

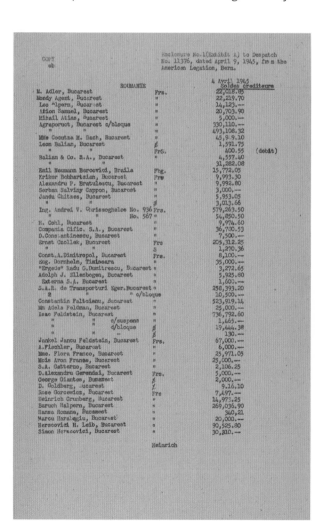

**Safehaven Report, April 9, 1945**
*National Archives, Records of the Office of the Judge Advocate General (Army)*

The Allies' effort to persuade neutral countries to seize German assets deposited in their countries was code-named Operation Safehaven. Safehaven documents in the National Archives are among those that have brought to light information about assets stolen from Holocaust victims. This page lists individuals, most of whom were Jewish, who tried to hide money from the Nazis by depositing it in Swiss bank accounts. The accounts were untouched between 1942 and 1945, and their owners probably perished in the Holocaust.

opposite page (bottom):
**Totenbuch Mauthausen (Mauthausen Death Book) March 27, 1942**
*National Archives, National Archives Collection of World War II War Crimes Records*

This page from Austria's Mauthausen concentration camp's "Death Book" lists names, national or ethnic origin, birth date, birthplace, and cause and time of death of the victims. Most often the cause of death was attributed to various medical ailments, although the last column on the right, reserved for "remarks," documents the deaths of prisoners "shot while attempting to escape" and "suicide [by jumping] in the quarry."

*Diese banditen verteidigten sich mit den Waffen.*

**Photograph from the Stroop Report, April–May 1943**
*National Archives, National Archives Collection of World War II War Crimes Records*

To document his brutal suppression of the Jewish uprising in the Warsaw Ghetto, April 20 to May 15, 1943, SS commander Jürgen Stroop created a final report that included a list of casualties incurred by his troops plus fifty hand-captioned photographs. The caption for this photograph from the report translates as "These bandits offered armed resistance."

## U.S. Senate Select Committee on Presidential Campaign Activities: Watergate

On July 17, 1972, burglars were caught inside the Watergate, a Washington, DC, building complex, attempting to bug the offices of the Democratic National Committee. Congress and the Justice Department investigated the break-in. In February 1973, amid growing suspicion that there was more to the break-in, the Senate established an investigative committee headed by Senator Sam Ervin, Jr., to look into what was becoming the Watergate scandal. The Senate committee began by focusing on the break-in and its cover-up but then discovered other illegal and improper actions aimed at opponents of the Nixon administration.

**Security officer's log of the Watergate office building, June 17, 1972**
*National Archives, Records of the Watergate Special Prosecution Force*

On this page from a log kept by the Watergate's guard force, security officer Frank Wills recorded the events of the break-in. During his checks, Wills discovered tape on doors that he had previously secured. He called Washington, DC, police, who arrested five men discovered in the office. The entries read: "[Left] 1:47 A.M. [Returned] 1:55 A.M. Call police found tape on doors. Call police two. Make a inspection on the inspection."

THE WHITE HOUSE
WASHINGTON

August 9, 1974

Dear Mr. Secretary:

I hereby resign the Office of President of the
United States.

Sincerely,

*Richard Nixon*

11.35 A.M.

HK

The Honorable Henry A. Kissinger
The Secretary of State
Washington, D.C. 20520

below:

**Address book of Watergate burglar Bernard Barker, discovered in a room at the Watergate Hotel, June 18, 1972**
*National Archives, Records of the District Courts of the United States*

Investigators searched the Watergate burglars' hotel rooms on June 18, 1972, and discovered Bernard Barker's phonebook. Barker's address book lists an entry for "HH," or Howard Hunt, a contractor who worked for the White House. The "WH" next to Hunt's phone number helped investigators connect the break-in to the White House and President Richard M. Nixon's reelection campaign.

above:

**Letter of resignation from President Richard Nixon to Secretary of State Henry Kissinger, August 9, 1974**
*National Archives, General Records of the Department of State*

Facing impeachment and removal from office, President Nixon resigned on August 9, 1974. Four days earlier Nixon had released three tapes that implicated him in the cover-up. By law the President or Vice President must submit their written resignation to the Secretary of State. At 11:35 A.M. on August 9, 1974, Secretary of State Henry Kissinger initialed Nixon's resignation letter signaling the end of the thirty-seventh President's second term.

Each year the President of the United States, members of Congress, and officials of Federal agencies collectively receive millions of letters from American citizens and people around the world. The correspondence covers a broad range of topics and records wide-ranging opinions and perspectives. Many writers want information or advice. Others ask a favor or state an opinion. The tone of the letters varies widely; some are filled with praise, while others express outrage, sadness, or humor. Communication is sometimes presented in creative and unexpected ways. As a whole, the voluminous correspondence represents a lively dialogue between people enjoying freedom of speech and their government.

**Letter from unidentified sender, March 9, 1899**
*National Archives, General Records of the Department of the Treasury*

This anonymous letter to the Secretary of the Treasury was enclosed with one dollar to cover the cost of an extra loaf of bread taken thirty-six years earlier while the writer was serving in the army during the Civil War.

right:
**Pvt. Emory Eugene Kingin, 4th Michigan Infantry, 1861–65**
*National Archives, Records of the Office of the Chief Signal Officer (111-B-5348)*

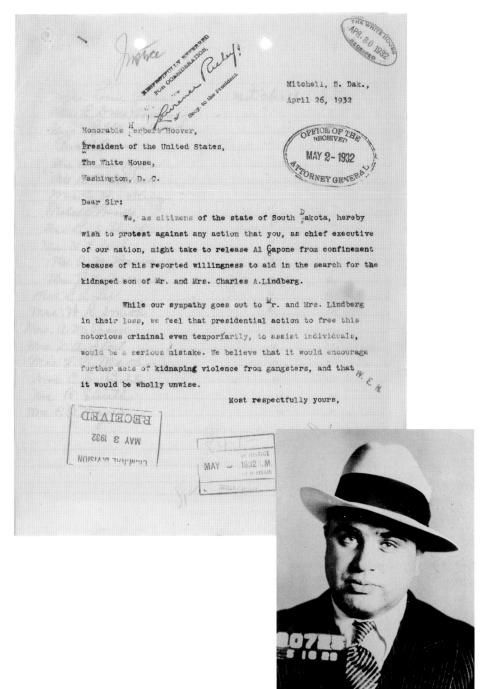

Mitchell, S. Dak.,
April 26, 1932

Honorable Herbert Hoover,
President of the United States,
The White House,
Washington, D. C.

Dear Sir:

We, as citizens of the state of South Dakota, hereby
wish to protest against any action that you, as chief executive
of our nation, might take to release Al Capone from confinement
because of his reported willingness to aid in the search for the
kidnaped son of Mr. and Mrs. Charles A.Lindberg.

While our sympathy goes out to Mr. and Mrs. Lindberg
in their loss, we feel that presidential action to free this
notorious criminal even temporarily, to assist individuals,
would be a serious mistake. We believe that it would encourage
further acts of kidnaping violence from gangsters, and that
it would be wholly unwise.

Most respectfully yours,

**Letter to President Herbert Hoover from citizens of South Dakota, April 26, 1932**
*National Archives, General Records of the Department of Justice*

When twenty-month-old Charles A. Lindbergh, Jr., son of aviator Charles Lindbergh and his wife, Anne Morrow Lindbergh, was kidnapped on March 1, 1932, some blamed organized crime. Al Capone—legendary symbol of the violent gangsterism of the Prohibition era, who was in jail on a charge of income-tax evasion—declared that he could find the gang responsible if he could be freed from prison for two weeks. Outrage at that idea elicited this April 26 letter from citizens of South Dakota to President Herbert Hoover. Capone's offer of assistance was ultimately rejected.

On May 12 the body of the stolen child was found about four and a half miles from the Lindbergh home. In 1934 police arrested Bruno Richard Hauptmann, who was charged with the murder.

**Al Capone, 1930**
*National Archives, Records of the United States Information Agency (306-NT-163.820c)*

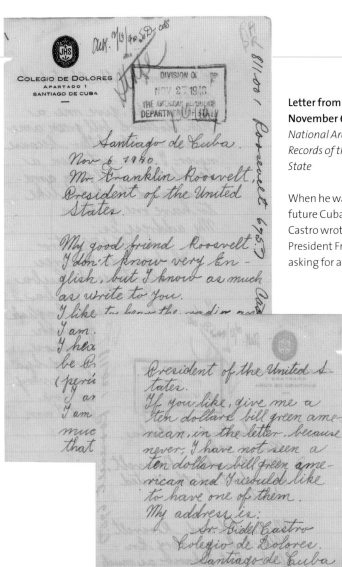

COLEGIO DE DOLORES
APARTADO 1
SANTIAGO DE CUBA

Santiago de Cuba.
Nov 6 1940.
Mr. Franklin Roosevelt,
President of the United
States.

My good friend Roosevelt
I don't know very En-
glish, but I know as much
as write to you.

President of the United S-
tates.
If you like, give me a
ten dollars bill green american, in the letter, because
never, I have not seen a
ten dollars bill green american and I would like
to have one of them.
My address is:
    Sr. Fidel Castro
    Colegio de Dolores.
    Santiago de Cuba.
    Oriente. Cuba.
I don't know very English
but I know very much
Spanish and I suppose
you don't know very Spa-
nish but you know very
English because you
are American but I am
not American.

(Thank you very much)
Good by. Your friend,

Fidel Castro

If you want iron to make
your ships I will
show to you the biggest
(minas) of iron of the land.
They are in Mayari. Oriente
Cuba.

**Letter from Fidel Castro,
November 6, 1940**
*National Archives, General
Records of the Department of
State*

When he was just 12 years old,
future Cuban President Fidel
Castro wrote a letter to
President Franklin D. Roosevelt
asking for a $10 bill.

bottom right:
**Cuban President Fidel Castro
in Havana, detail, 1963**
© AP/Wide World Photos
*National Archives, Records of
the U.S. Information Agency
(306-PSD-63-1158)*

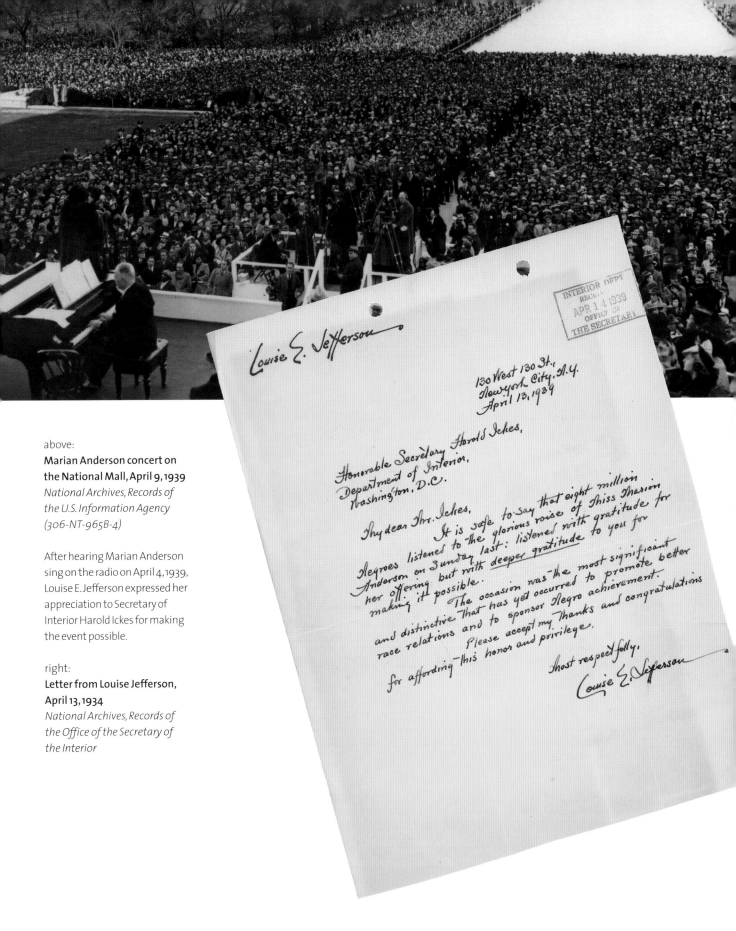

above:

**Marian Anderson concert on the National Mall, April 9, 1939**
*National Archives, Records of the U.S. Information Agency (306-NT-965B-4)*

After hearing Marian Anderson sing on the radio on April 4, 1939, Louise E. Jefferson expressed her appreciation to Secretary of Interior Harold Ickes for making the event possible.

right:

**Letter from Louise Jefferson, April 13, 1934**
*National Archives, Records of the Office of the Secretary of the Interior*

INTERIOR DEPT
REC'D
APR 1 4 1939
OFFICE OF
THE SECRETARY

Louise E. Jefferson

130 West 130 St.,
New York City. N.Y.
April 13, 1939

Honorable Secretary Harold Ickes,
Department of Interior,
Washington, D.C.

My dear Mr. Ickes,

It is safe to say that eight million Negroes listened to the glorious voice of Miss Marion Anderson on Sunday last: listened with gratitude for her offering but with *deeper gratitude* to you for making it possible. The occasion was the most significant and distinctive that has yet occurred to promote better race relations and to sponsor Negro achievement. Please accept my thanks and congratulations for affording this honor and privilege.

Most respectfully,
Louise E. Jefferson

The White House
Washington

FEB 24  6 18 AM 1942

PFF 200
RADIO ADDRESS
2 23

PRO "M"

WB83 26 NT

BRIDGEPORT CONN FEB 23

PRESIDENT ROOSEVELT

WHITE HOUSE

JUST HEARD YOUR SPEECH IT CHEERED ME UP RECEIVED NOTICE TODAY

THAT MY SON WAS KILLED IN SERVICE OF THE UNITEDSTATES AT

PEARL HARBOR DECEMBER 7TH

J B MANUAL.

opposite page (inset):
**Telegram from J. B. Manual, February 24, 1942**
*National Archives, Franklin D. Roosevelt Library*

In a telegram to President Franklin D. Roosevelt, J. B. Manual said he was cheered up after hearing Roosevelt's speech to the nation—delivered on the same day Mr. Manual learned his son had died in the Japanese attack on Pearl Harbor. On December 7, 1941, Japanese warplanes had attacked the home base of the U.S. Pacific fleet at Pearl Harbor, an act that led to America's entry into World War II.

main image:
**USS *Shaw* exploding during the Japanese raid on Pearl Harbor, December 7, 1941**
*National Archives, General Records of the Department of the Navy (80-G-16871)*

**President Franklin D. Roosevelt signing the declaration of war against Japan, December 8, 1941**
*National Archives, Records of the National Park Service (79-AR-82)*

**Letter from German school-children, 1948**
*National Archives, Harry S. Truman Library (3025)*

To thank the United States for a postwar program that provided lunches for German schoolchildren, a class of fifth graders from Pfaffenhofen, Germany, sent this hand-drawn letter to President Harry Truman in 1948.

opposite page:
**Letter from Ray Fadden, September 3, 1951**
*National Archives, Harry S. Truman Library*

In September 1951, Ray Fadden, secretary of the Akwesasne Mohawk Counselor Organization, thanked President Harry S. Truman for allowing Winnebago Indian Sgt. John R. Rice to be buried in Arlington Cemetery.

# Akwesasne Mohawk Counselor Organization

(KA NIN KE A KA — PEOPLE OF FLINT)

St. Regis Mohawk Reservation
Hogansburg, New York

Secretary
(Ra ia Tons)
Ray Fadden

Sept. 3, 1951

President Harry Truman
Washington, D.C.
White house

Dear President Truman,

The members of our Indian organization read of your
act as regards Sgt. John R. Rice who died in action in Korea.
We are ashamed that officials of Sioux City did the cruel
thing that they did, refusing to bury an Indian in their
cemetery. We were proud of you, Brother, when we read of
you allowing our warrior to be buried in the Arlington
...metery. We want you to know that we are grateful to you
...appreciate it very much. May the Great Spirit bless your
...ing one of our people.

Cordially yours,

Ray Fadden

Ray Fadden, Sec.

Members of Co. F, 2nd
Battalion, 7th Infantry
Regiment, 3rd U.S. Infantry
Division, Korea, December 5,
1952
*National Archives, Records of
the Office of the Chief Signal
Officer (111-C-7746)*

Received SS
1984 MAY -9 AM 10: 36

Andy Smith
400 London Pride Road
Irmo, South Carolina 29063

April 18, 1984

Dear Mr. President,

My name is Andy Smith. I am a seventh grade student at Irmo
Middle School, in Irmo, South Carolina.

Today my mother declared my bedroom a disaster area. I would like
to request federal funds to hire a crew to clean up my room. I am
prepared to provide the initial funds if you will privide matching funds
for this project.

I know you will be fair when you consider my request. I will be
awaiting your reply.

Sincerely yours,

Andy Smith
Andy Smith

**Letter from Andy Smith to
President Reagan, April 18, 1984**
*National Archives, Ronald
Reagan Library*

below:
**Letter from President Reagan
to Andy Smith, 1984**
*National Archives, Ronald
Reagan Library*

below:
**President Reagan during a
meeting with members of
Congress, November 1, 1983**
*National Archives, Ronald
Reagan Library (C18011-24)*

In April 1984, stating that his
mother had designated his
bedroom a disaster area, seventh
grader Andy Smith asked
President Ronald Reagan for
Federal funds to clean it up. In
response, President Reagan
suggested that Andy start a
"Private Sector Initiative
Program" and find volunteers
to assist in his relief effort.

To Andy Smith 400 London Pride Rd.
Irmo So. Carolina 29063

Dear Andy

I'm sorry to be so late in answering your
letter but as you know I've been in China and
found your letter here upon my return.

Your application for disaster relief has been
duly noted but I must point out one technical
problem; the authority declaring the disaster is supposed
to make the request. In this case your mother.

However setting that aside I'll have to point
out the larger problem of available funds. This
has been a year of disasters, 539 hurricanes as of
May 4th and several more since, numerous floods,
forest fires, drought in Texas and a number of
earthquakes. What I'm getting at is that funds are
dangerously low.

May I make a suggestion? This administration,
believing that govt. has done many things that
could better be done by volunteers at the local level,
has sponsored a Private Sector Initiative Program,
calling upon people to practice voluntarism in the
solving of a number of local problems.

Your situation appears to be a natural. I'm sure
your Mother was fully justified in proclaiming your
room a disaster. Therefore you are in an excellent
position to launch another volunteer program to go along
with the more than 3000 already underway in our nation.
Congratulations.

Give my best regards to your Mother

Sincerely Ronald Reagan

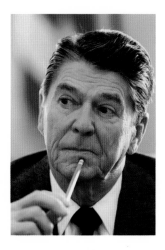

```
==================== ATTACHMENT  1 ====================
ATT CREATION TIME/DATE:   0 00:00:00.00

TEXT:
From margie.s.keller1@jsc.nasa.gov  Fri Nov  6 15:44:27 1998
Received: (from uucp@localhost) by WhiteHouse.gov (8.7.1/uucp-relay) id PAA1941
5 for ; Fri, 6 Nov 1998 15:44:27 -0500 (EST)
Received: from storm.eop.gov/198.137.241.51 via smap
Return-receipt-to: "KELLER, MARGIE S. (JSC-CB)"

Received: from DIRECTORY-DAEMON by STORM.EOP.GOV (PMDF V5.1-12 #29131)
 id <01J3UX518GIO000XPO@STORM.EOP.GOV> for President@WhiteHouse.GOV; Fri,
 6 Nov 1998 15:43:11 EST
Received: from SCAN-DAEMON by STORM.EOP.GOV (PMDF V5.1-12 #29131)
 id <01J3UX4ZT0OC0000X6@STORM.EOP.GOV> for president@Whitehouse.GOV; Fri,
 06 Nov 1998 15:43:09 -0500 (EST)
Received: from jsc-ems-gws03.jsc.nasa.gov ([139.169.39.19])
 by STORM.EOP.GOV (PMDF V5.1-12 #29131)
 with ESMTP id <01J3UX4R0VHW000XUJ@STORM.EOP.GOV> for president@Whitehouse.GOV;

 Fri, 06 Nov 1998 15:43:01 -0500 (EST)
Received: by jsc-ems-gws03.jsc.nasa.gov with Internet Mail Service (5.5.2232.9)

 id ; Fri, 06 Nov 1998 14:43:06 -0600
Content-return: allowed
Date: Fri, 06 Nov 1998 14:42:56 -0600
From: "KELLER, MARGIE S. (JSC-CB)"
Subject: STS-95 Downlink Mail
To: "'president@whitehouse.gov'"
Message-id:
 <81F639B56628D011A32D0020AFFC01900231E72D@jsc-ems-mbs07.jsc.nasa.gov>
MIME-version: 1.0
X-Mailer: Internet Mail Service (5.5.2232.9)
Content-type: MULTIPART/MIXED; BOUNDARY="Boundary_(ID_4wKF5vI8SCrlrTB4D1H6vg)"

Importance: high
Comments: This message scanned by SCAN version 0.1 jms/960226
X-Priority: 1


--Boundary_(ID_4wKF5vI8SCrlrTB4D1H6vg)
Content-type: TEXT/PLAIN; CHARSET=US-ASCII
Content-transfer-encoding: 7BIT

President Bill Clinton, The White House, Washington, D. C.

Dear Mr. President,
        This is  certainly a first for me, writing to a President from space,
and it may be a first for you in receiving an E mail direct from an orbiting
spacecraft.

        In any event, I want to personally thank you and  Mrs. Clinton for
coming to the Cape to see the launch.  I hope you enjoyed  it just half as
much as we did on board.. It is truly an awesome experience from a personal
standpoint, and of even greater importance for all of the great research
projects we have on Discovery.  The whole crew was impressed that you would
be the first President to personally see a shuttle launch and asked me to
include their best regards to you and  Hillary.   She has discussed her
interest in the space program with Annie on several occasions, and I know
she would like to be on a flight just like this.

        We have gone   almost a third of  the way  around the world in the time
it has taken me to write this letter, and the rest of the crew is waiting.
Again, our thanks and best regards.  Will  try to give you a personal
briefing after we return next Saturday.


   Sincerely,

                       John Glenn

Margie S. Keller
Admin Officer
Astronaut Office
281-244-8991

--Boundary_(ID_4wKF5vI8SCrlrTB4D1H6vg)--

==================== END ATTACHMENT  1 ====================
```

The Space Shuttle *Challenger*,
1983
*National Archives, Records of
the U.S. Information Agency
(306-PSE-83-2622cA)*

In November 1998, Senator and
former astronaut John Glenn
e-mailed President Bill Clinton
to thank him for the opportunity to return to space at age 77.

left:
**E-mail from Senator John
Glenn to President Clinton,
November 6, 1998**
*National Archives, William J.
Clinton Library*

THE PUBLIC VAULTS UNLOCKED

Approved by the Continental Congress on June 20, 1782, the Great Seal of the United States is a symbol of America's sovereignty as a nation. Kept by the Secretary of State, the Great Seal is used to authenticate the signature of the President. Appearing on proclamations, warrants, treaties, and commissions of Government officials, the imprint of the Great Seal is one key to proving that a record is authentic.

The Great Seal is the result of the three committees and fourteen individuals who worked for six years to complete the design. Some of America's greatest minds were involved in the project, including Thomas Jefferson, Benjamin Franklin, and John Adams. None, however, left a more lasting impression than Secretary of the Continental Congress Charles Thomson, who distilled the work of previous contributors to create the seal as we know it.

**Francis Hopkinson's first and second designs for the Great Seal, May 1780**
*National Archives, Records of the Continental and Confederation Congresses and the Constitutional Convention*

In the spring of 1780, the second Great Seal committee consulted Francis Hopkinson, designer of the American flag and a signer of the Declaration of Independence. He introduced the thirteen red and white stripes on the shield, the constellation of thirteen stars, the thirteen arrows, and the olive branch with thirteen olives—all on the front of the seal.

The third committee to design the Great Seal met on May 4, 1782, and consulted William Barton, a student of heraldry. His designs, completed five days later, incorporated the eagle for the first time (see p. 18 for his design for the Seal's front). Barton's designs were sent to Congress for approval early the next month.

Back     Front

Hopkinson's first design

Back     Front

Hopkinson's second design

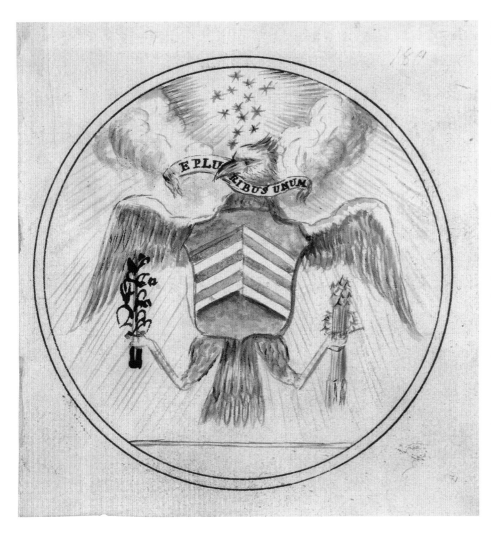

**Charles Thomson's design for the Great Seal (front only), June 1782**

*National Archives, Records of the Continental and Confederation Congresses and the Constitutional Convention*

On the front of the fourth design, Charles Thomson combined elements of all three previous attempts to complete the final design for the Great Seal in June 1782. Thomson made the eagle, with its wings pointed down as if in flight, the focal point. The shield on the eagle's breast was blue with thirteen red and white chevrons pointing up. In his report to Congress, Thomson described the Seal and its symbolism, explaining in part, "The thirteen pieces … represent the several states in the Union all joined in one solid compact entire, supporting a Chief, which unites the whole and represents Congress," and "The colours … are those used in the flag of the United States of America; White signifies purity and innocence; Red, hardiness and valour, and Blue, the colour of the Chief, signifies vigilance, perseverance, and justice."

above:
**First Die of the Great Seal of the United States, September 1782**
*National Archives, General Records of the U.S. Government*

When designing the first die for the Great Seal, William Barton interpreted Charles Thomson's report. He changed the stripes of the shield from chevron to vertical, and the bald eagle to a crested eagle. On September 16, 1782, this brass die of the front of the Great Seal was first used to impress its engraved design onto softer metals. Notice that it features a crested eagle instead of today's bald eagle. This die was used until 1841. A die of the reverse side was never cut.

**Percy F. Allen, Assistant to the Chief Clerk and Chief of the Appointment Section, Department of State, using the Great Seal press, ca. 1924–39**
*Photograph courtesy of the U.S. Department of State*

# MAKE YOUR OWN SEAL

Design your own Great Seal of the United States (see representation of current Great Seal die below) by tracing, copying, and then coloring elements from this page. Do you want to include a glory, a motto, a shield, an eagle, an olive branch, and arrows? Combine the elements in personal ways. As you color, consider what the colors mean. Feel free to add other designs and symbols, too. What ideas to you want to convey? Strength? Courage? Unity? What objects would you select to symbolize those ideas? You can make other seals, too. Consider making a seal for your school or family. What symbols would you choose?

**The Great Seal today (front)**
*Created by the U.S. Department of State*

PROVINCIAL COMPANY, NEW YORK ARTILLERY, CAPTAIN ALEXANDER HAMILTON
1776.

# PROVIDE FOR THE COMMON DEFENSE

## RECORDS OF THE MILITARY AND DIPLOMACY

The National Archives takes special pride in its role in preserving the records of those who have protected the United States. America's military and diplomatic records paint a vivid picture of heroism, inspiration, and sacrifice. Military records held by the National Archives include those for individuals and units in all branches of the military.

top row, left to right: **Marine, U.S. Marine Corps, Peleliu Island, Palau Islands, 1944,** *National Archives, General Records of the Department of the Navy, 1798–1947 (80-G-48358);* **Capt. Alexander Hamilton, Provincial Company, New York Artillery, Revolutionary War, 1776, watercolor by D.W.C. Falls, 1923,** *National Archives, Records of U.S. Regular Army Mobile Units (391-AR-2-1);* **Marine, 3rd Battalion, 1st Marine Regiment, U.S. Marine Corps, near Da Nang, Vietnam, ca. 1965,** *National Archives, Records of the U.S. Marine Corps (127-N-A374394);* **National Standard of the 1st Cavalry, ca. 1898,** *National Archives, Records of the Office of the Chief Signal Officer (111-SC-89743)*

middle row, left to right: **Unidentified pilot, 91st Aero Squadron, U.S. Army, France, 1919,** *National Archives, Records of the Army Air Forces (18E-5228);* **Fireman 1st Class Marvin Sanders, U.S. Coast Guard, Southwest Pacific, ca. 1942,** *National Archives, Records of the Office of War Information (208-NP-8WWW-8);* **Scout Tsoe (Peaches), U.S. Army, 1885,** *National Archives, Records of the Office of*

the Chief Signal Officer (111-SC-82346); **Lt. Margaret Stanfill, 120th Evacuation Hospital, U.S. Army, Normandy, France, 1944,** *National Archives, Records of the Office of the Chief Signal Officer (111-SC-190305);* **Pfc. Russell R. Widdifield, 3rd Battalion, 7th Marine Regiment, U.S. Marine Corps, near An Hoa, Vietnam, ca. 1965,** *National Archives, Records of the U.S. Marine Corps (127-N-A374601)*

bottom row, left to right: **Pfc. Edith Macies, U.S. Marine Corps, Washington, DC, 1919,** *National Archives, Records of the War Department General and Special Staffs (165-WW598A-10);* **Lt. Gen. Thomas J. "Stonewall" Jackson, Confederate States of America, by George W. Minnes, 1863,** *National Archives, Records of the Office of the Chief Signal Officer (111-B-1867);* **S./Sgt. James S. Kawashime, 442nd Regimental Combat Team, U.S. Army, Charmois, France, 1944,** *National Archives, Records of the Office of the Chief Signal Officer (111-SC-212248)*

ENTER>

**Drummer boy Taylor, 78th Regiment, U.S. Colored Infantry, ca. 1863**

*National Archives, Records of the War Department General and Special Staffs (165-JT-302)*

Marine, 3rd Marine Division,
U.S. Marine Corps, Da Nang,
Vietnam, 1965
*National Archives, Records of
the U.S. Marine Corps (127-GVC-
40-A185146)*

## I WANT YOU!

The United States has a tradition of volunteer military service. As times and cultures have changed, the uniformed services have come up with novel and diverse ways of encouraging citizens to sign up. Posters, billboards, short movies, newsreels, and TV commercials have all helped attract male and female recruits. Sometimes, however—particularly in times of war—the Government has resorted to selective drafts to reach the authorized force level. When conscription has occurred, it has been opposed by some citizens. Today, even without a draft, all men must register for selective service at age 18.

**Civilians line up to enroll in U.S. Navy flight training during World War II, ca. 1941**
*National Archives, General Records of the Department of the Navy, 1798–1947 (80-G-060481)*

right:
**Draft Registration Card for Louis Armstrong, 1917**
*National Archives, Records of the Selective Service System (World War I)*

Future jazz great Louis Armstrong of New Orleans was among nearly 24 million men aged 18 to 45 who registered for the draft in 1917 and 1918, a requirement of the new Selective Service System. Notice that his first name is given incorrectly as "Lewis." And while his date of birth was recorded as July 4, 1900, Armstrong was actually born on August 4, 1901.

below:

**"Oath of Enlistment and Allegiance" for Bull Eagle (Indian Scout), 1874**
*National Archives, Records of the Adjutant General's Office, 1780's–1917*

In 1866, Congress had authorized the enlistment in the U.S. military of up to 1,000 Indian scouts, most of whom joined the army to help track rival tribes. By signing this document on August 21, 1874, Bull Eagle of the Lakota Sioux enlisted as a scout with the 11th Infantry Regiment during the Plains Indians Wars. On line two he listed his occupation as "hunter." Unlike soldiers, scouts typically enlisted for only six months.

below right:

**"Men Wanted for the Army," poster by Michael P. Whelan, ca. 1908**
*National Archives, Records of the Adjutant General's Office, 1780's–1917 (94-WP-19)*

## Recruiting Posters

Powerful visual tools, recruiting posters have been used for centuries to convince citizens to serve their country. Early recruiting posters were printed notices, mostly composed of words but sometimes bearing black-and-white illustrations. By the late nineteenth century, however, posters printed in color showed servicemen in dashing uniforms striking gallant poses in exotic locations. During the twentieth century, posters from the two world wars used patriotic appeals and images of female seductiveness and male heroics as recruiting tools.

After World War II, enlistment appeals became more practical. Serving in the military was presented as a smart way to learn marketable skills and a fast track to professional advancement.

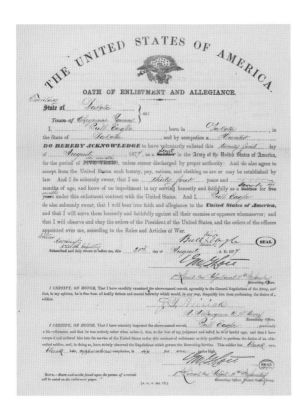

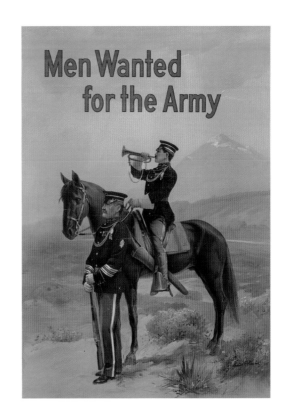

## REPORTS FROM THE FRONT

In times of war, dramatic events have been documented by men and women serving in the field—even during battle. Deck logs, battalion diaries, staff duty journals, and communications within and between units are some examples of military accounts composed by people who may not have thought of themselves as historians or even history makers. Yet first-person documentation of military engagements, frequently prepared by men and women in the course of their daily duties, comprise some of the most compelling historic records in the National Archives. Often written before the outcome of the battle or war was known, reports from the front convey the urgency felt by participants in the midst of combat.

S.S. BALTIC. OFF SANDY HOOK APR. EIGHTEENTH. TEN THIRTY A.M. .VIA NEW YORK. . HON. S. CAMERON. SECY. WAR. WASHN. HAVING DEFENDED FORT SUMTER FOR THIRTY FOUR HOURS UNTIL THE QUARTERS WERE ENTIRELY BURNED THE MAIN GATES DESTROYED BY FIRE. THE GORGE WALLS SERIOUSLY INJURED. THE MAGAZINE SURROUNDED BY FLAMES AND ITS DOOR CLOSED FROM THE EFFECTS OF HEAT . FOUR BARRELLS AND THREE CARTRIDGES OF POWDER ONLY BEING AVAILABLE AND NO PROVISIONS REMAINING BUT PORK. I ACCEPTED TERMS OF EVACUATION OFFERED BY GENERAL BEAUREGARD BEING ON SAME OFFERED BY HIM ON THE ELEVENTH INST. PRIOR TO THE COMMENCEMENT OF HOSTILITIES AND MARCHED OUT OF THE FORT SUNDAY AFTERNOON THE FOURTEENTH INST. WITH COLORS FLYING AND DRUMS BEATING. BRINGING AWAY COMPANY AND PRIVATE PROPERTY AND SALUTING MY FLAG WITH FIFTY GUNS. ROBERT ANDERSON. MAJOR FIRST ARTILLERY. COMMANDING.

**Telegram from Maj. Robert Anderson to Secretary of War Simon Cameron, reporting the fall of Fort Sumter, April 18, 1861**
*National Archives, Records of the Adjutant General's Office, 1780's–1917*

This telegram notified Secretary of War Simon Cameron of the outcome of the battle that began the Civil War in earnest and ended the possibility of a peaceful resolution between the Union and the Confederacy. The battle of Fort Sumter, in Charleston Harbor, South Carolina, started at 4:30 A.M. on April 12, 1861, when Maj. Robert Anderson, commander of the Union garrison there, refused to surrender it to Confederate Brig. Gen. Pierre G. T. Beauregard, commander of Confederate forces at Charleston. The battle for Fort Sumter ended with Anderson's surrender after thirty-four hours. Anderson evacuated the garrison and sailed for New York, sending the telegram five days later.

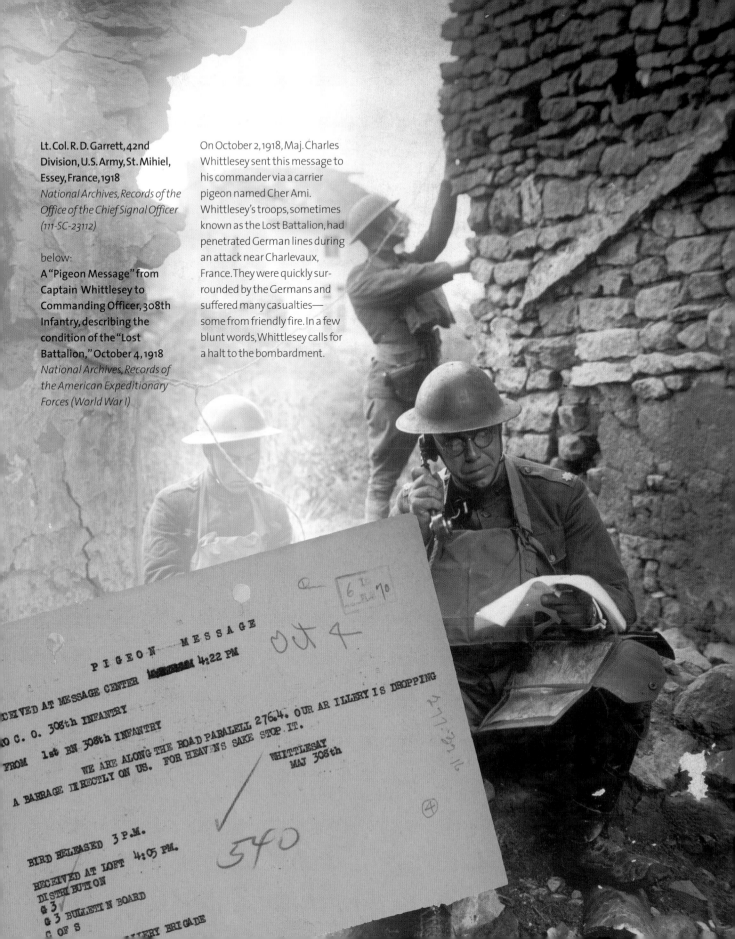

Lt. Col. R. D. Garrett, 42nd Division, U.S. Army, St. Mihiel, Essey, France, 1918
*National Archives, Records of the Office of the Chief Signal Officer (111-SC-23112)*

below:
A "Pigeon Message" from Captain Whittlesey to Commanding Officer, 308th Infantry, describing the condition of the "Lost Battalion," October 4, 1918
*National Archives, Records of the American Expeditionary Forces (World War I)*

On October 2, 1918, Maj. Charles Whittlesey sent this message to his commander via a carrier pigeon named Cher Ami. Whittlesey's troops, sometimes known as the Lost Battalion, had penetrated German lines during an attack near Charlevaux, France. They were quickly surrounded by the Germans and suffered many casualties—some from friendly fire. In a few blunt words, Whittlesey calls for a halt to the bombardment.

PIGEON MESSAGE

RECEIVED AT MESSAGE CENTER 4:22 PM

TO C. O. 308th INFANTRY

FROM 1st BN 308th INFANTRY

WE ARE ALONG THE ROAD PARALELL 276.4. OUR ARTILLERY IS DROPPING A BARRAGE DIRECTLY ON US. FOR HEAVENS SAKE STOP IT.

WHITTLESAY
MAJ 308th

BIRD RELEASED 3 P.M.

RECEIVED AT LOFT 4:05 PM.

DISTRIBUTION
G 3
G 3 BULLETIN BOARD
C OF S

# CITATIONS

Military records in the National Archives relate stories of incredible bravery on the battlefield. Recommendations for a Medal of Honor or other awards for valor recount actions above and beyond the call of duty. They detail, for example, the actions taken by men and women trying to save their friends by jumping on grenades, fighting desperate rear-guard actions, or single-handedly destroying enemy positions. In many cases, the recommendations are for posthumous awards.

Award recommendations are submitted on standard forms that belie the heroic stories they chronicle. The National Archives preserves thousands of records honoring those who have served their country well.

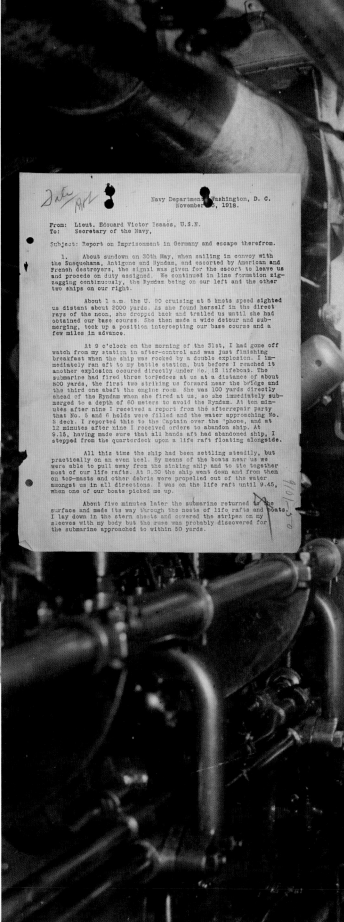

**Pfc. Edward M. Palya receiving the Silver Star, July 5, 1944**
*National Archives, Records of the Office of the Chief Signal Officer (111-SC-312818)*

above right (inset):
**"Report on German imprisonment in Germany and escape therefrom," by Lt. Edouard Isaacs, 1918**
Page 1
*National Archives, Records of the Bureau of Naval Personnel*

## Medal of Honor citation for Lt. Edouard Victor Michel Isaacs, U.S. Navy, by the Secretary of the Navy, ca. 1919

Excerpt from transcription
*National Archives, Records of the Bureau of Naval Personnel*

*When the USS* President Lincoln *was attacked and sunk by the German Submarine U-90 on May 21st, 1918, Lieutenant Isaacs was captured and held as a prisoner on board the U-90 until the return of the Submarine to Germany, when he was confined in a prison camp. During his stay on the U-90 he obtained information of the movements of German Submarines, which was so important that he determined to escape with a view to making this information available to the United States and Allied Naval authorities. In attempting to carry out this plan, he jumped through the window of a rapidly moving train at the imminent risk of death, not only from the nature of the act itself but from the fire of the armed German soldiers who were guarding him. Having been recaptured and reconfined, he made a second and successful attempt to escape, breaking his way through barbed wire fences and deliberately drawing the fire of the armed guards in the hope of permitting others to escape during the confusion. He made his way through the mountains of southwestern Germany, having only raw vegetables for food and at the end swam the river Rhine during the night in the immediate vicinity of German sentries.*

main image:
**Engine room of an oil-burning German submarine, German Official, ca. 1919**
*National Archives, Records of the War Department General and Special Staffs (165-GB-2146)*

left (inset):
**Medal of Honor recipient Edouard Victor Michel Isaacs, December 18, 1918**
*National Archives, Records of the Bureau of Ships (19-N-12989)*

## Medal of Honor citation for S./Sgt. Clifford Chester Sims, U.S. Army, by Gen. William Westmoreland, December 12, 1969

Excerpt from transcription
*National Archives, Records of U.S. Forces in Southeast Asia, 1950–1975*

*Company D* [2d Battalion (Airborne), 501st Infantry, 101st Airborne Division] *was assaulting a heavily fortified enemy position* [near Hue, Republic of Vietnam] *concealed within a dense wooded area when it encountered strong enemy defensive fire. Once within the woodline* [sic], *Sergeant Sims led his squad in a furious attack against an enemy force which had pinned down the 1st Platoon and threatened to overrun it. His skillful leadership provided the platoon with freedom of movement and enabled it to regain the initiative.*

*Sergeant Sims was then ordered to move his squad to a position where he could provide covering fire for the company command group and to link up with the 3rd Platoon, which was under heavy enemy pressure. After moving no more than 30 meters, Sergeant Sims noticed that a brick structure in which ammunition was stocked was on fire. Realizing the danger, Sergeant Sims took immediate action to move his squad from this position. Though in the process of leaving the area two members of his squad were injured by the subsequent explosion of the ammunition, Sergeant Sims' prompt actions undoubtedly prevented more serious casualties from occurring.*

*While continuing through the dense woods amidst heavy enemy fire, Sergeant Sims and his squad were approaching a bunker when they heard the unmistakable noise of a concealed booby trap being triggered immediately to their front. Sergeant Sims warned his comrades of the danger and unhesitatingly hurled himself upon the device as it exploded, taking the full impact of the blast. In so protecting his fellow soldiers, he willingly sacrificed his life. Sergeant Sims' conspicuous gallantry, extraordinary hero-*

*ism and intrepidity at the cost of his own life, above and beyond the call of duty, are in keeping with the highest traditions of the military service and reflect great credit upon himself and the United States Army.*

**Medal of Honor recipient Clifford Chester Sims, ca. 1968**
*National Archives, Records of the Office of the Chief Signal Officer (111-PP-16795)*

opposite page:
**Eyewitness account of Sgt. Robert Washington, et al., re: Clifford Chester Sims, March 12, 1968**
*National Archives, Records of the U.S. Forces in Southeast Asia, 1950–1975*

EYEWITNESS STATEMENT

On 21 February 1968 Sgt Sims' squad was supporting elements of Co D 2/501st in an assault on enemy positions. He led his squad in providing fire power to cover the company commander as he crossed a wide expanse of open rice paddy. Sgt Sims then led his own men across under very heavy enemy fire and assaulted the enemy position in the woods to relieve pressure from the 1st Platoon which was pinned down. He was then ordered to move to the right to help the 3rd Platoon, and as the squad advanced Sgt Sims shot and killed two enemy soldiers, one of whom attacked him. He also saved his squad by moving them quickly out of the way of a house filled with ammunition which was burning. Just as he got his men away the house blew up. Then on moving toward a bunker a booby trap was set off, and Sgt Sims yelled for everybody to get back, but before they could he threw himself on the device taking the entire blast to save his squad from complete disaster. In so doing he gave up his own life. Each and every man of the 2nd Squad owes his very life to this man, Staff Sergeant Clifford C. Sims.

The above account is agreed to and testified as true by the undersigned:

SGT ROBERT WASHINGTON
Fire Team Leader

SP4 LARRY R. ACRA
Fire Team Leader

PVT RUFUS E. LUCUS
Rifleman

PFC LESTER H. HEISERMAN
Rifleman

PFC SALVATORE BONGIORNO
Rifleman

SP4 DAVID TROUTMAN
Fire Team Leader

SGT GARY O. PARNELL
Weapons Squad Leader

On July 18, 1863, the 54th Massachusetts Infantry Regiment led an assault of 6,000 Union troops on Fort Wagner, near Charleston, South Carolina. The fort was defended by 1,000 Confederates and the guns of Battery Gregg and Fort Sumter. The "Colored" 54th Regiment—with its white officers, including the commander, Col. Robert G. Shaw, and African American enlisted men, among them Sgt. Maj. Lewis H. Douglass, son of abolitionist Frederick Douglass—captured the fort's outer works. An hour later the Union troops were forced to fall back. One-hundred seventy-four Confederate troops and 1,515 Union troops were killed or wounded. Sgt. William H. Carney, who carried the regimental colors onto the parapet, was later awarded the Medal of Honor.

Records held in the National Archives provide a way to compare the historical record with the drama in films such as *Glory*, made in 1989. Directed by Edward Zwick, *Glory* portrays the 54th Massachusetts and its heroic attack on Fort Wagner. The film follows the regiment from its formation, through the training of its recruits, to the battle of Fort Wagner. While *Glory* accurately describes many of the social issues and obstacles faced by the men of the 54th, as in most feature films some of the events and characters were fictionalized to tell a broad story and heighten the drama.

**Map of Morris Island, 1863**
*National Archives, Records of the Adjutant General's Office, 1780's–1917*

This map of Morris Island, South Carolina, showing Confederate and Union positions around Fort Wagner, illustrates why it was so difficult to take Fort Wagner. Stretching across nearly the entire width of the island, the fort is located three-quarters of the way up the island when approached from the southwest, as the Union forces did. Assaulting troops could not bypass the strongpoint and had to conduct a frontal attack.

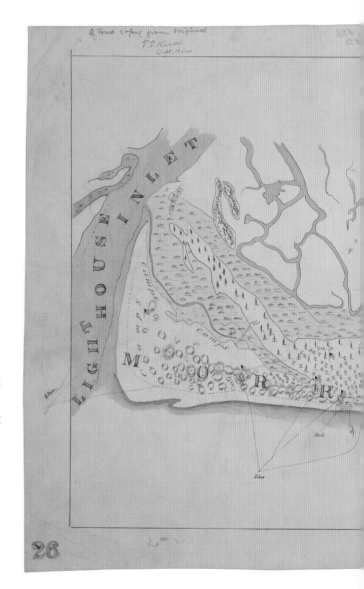

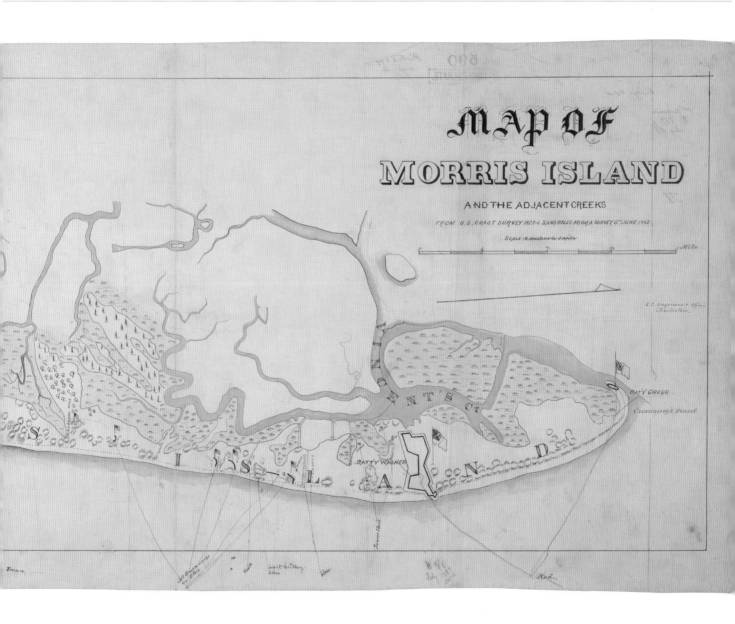

# MAP OF
## MORRIS ISLAND
### AND THE ADJACENT CREEKS

FROM U.S. COAST SURVEY 1823-4 SANDHILLS FROM A SURVEY 6TH JUNE 1862

Scale 8 inches to 1 mile

Mile

C.S. Engineer's Office
Charleston

BATY GREGG

Cumming's Point

BATTY WAGNER

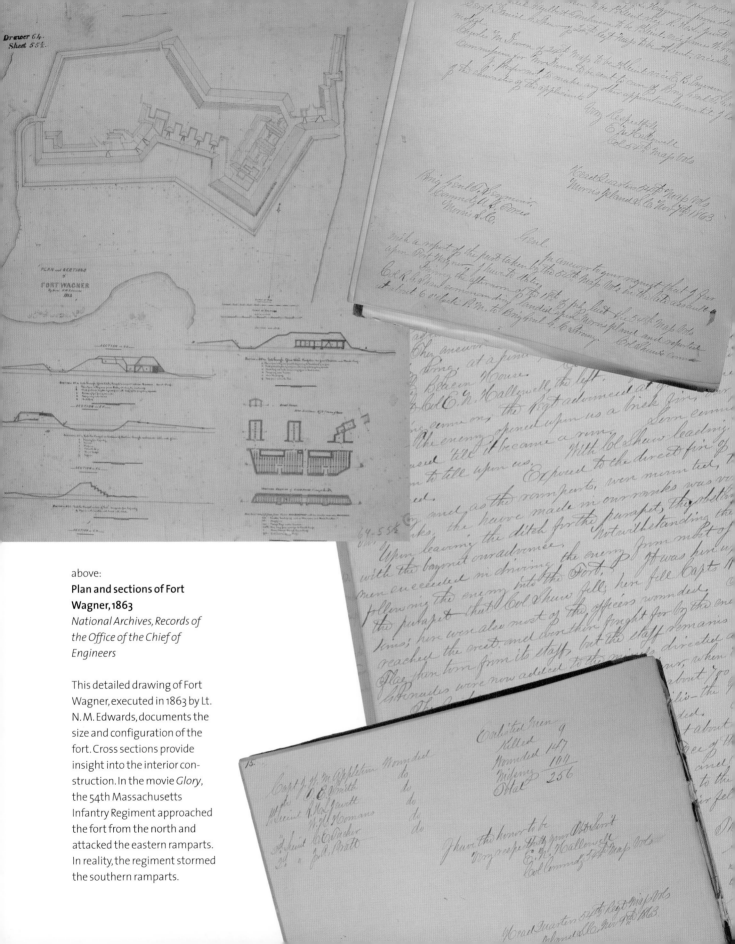

above:

**Plan and sections of Fort Wagner, 1863**

*National Archives, Records of the Office of the Chief of Engineers*

This detailed drawing of Fort Wagner, executed in 1863 by Lt. N. M. Edwards, documents the size and configuration of the fort. Cross sections provide insight into the interior construction. In the movie *Glory*, the 54th Massachusetts Infantry Regiment approached the fort from the north and attacked the eastern ramparts. In reality, the regiment stormed the southern ramparts.

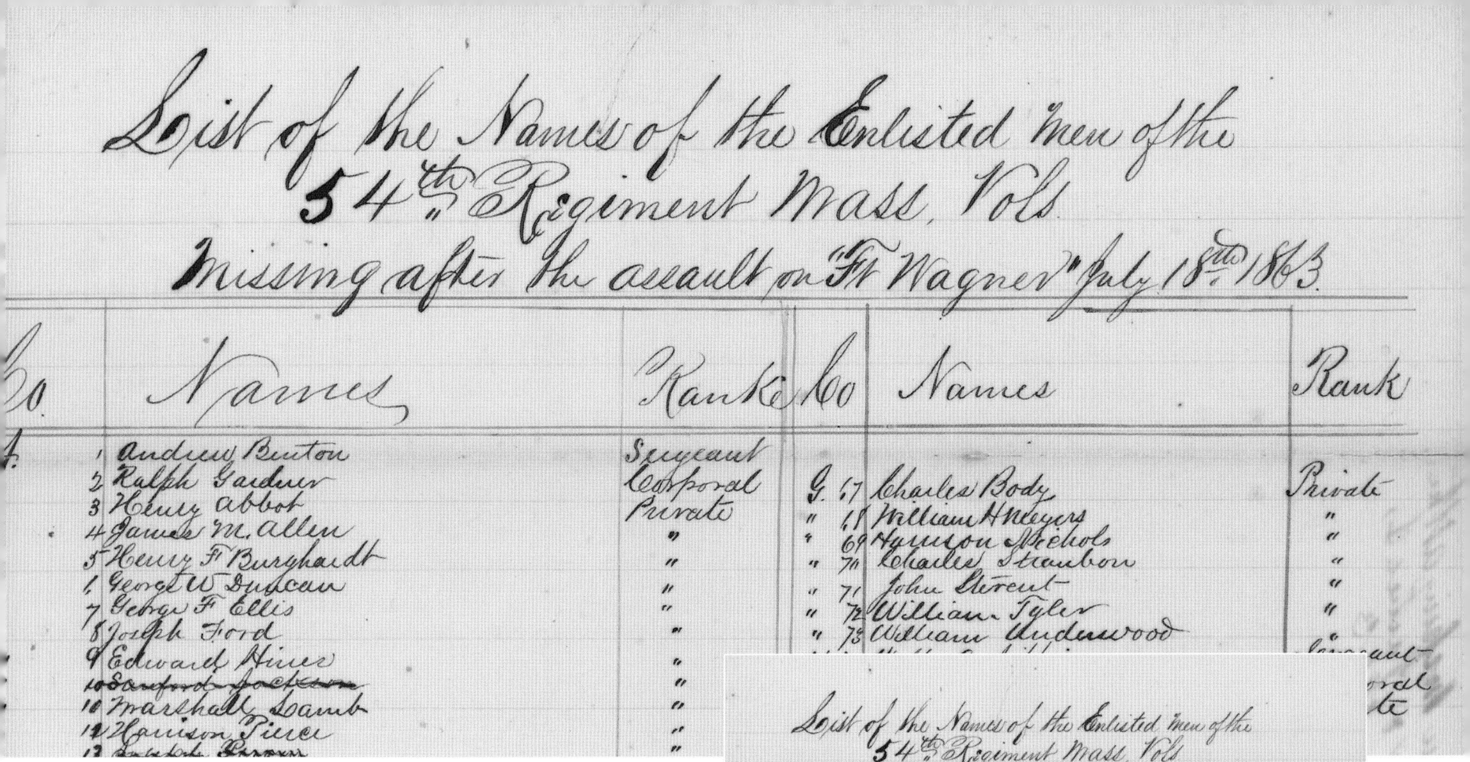

List of the Names of the Enlisted men of the
54th Regiment Mass. Vols
Missing after the assault on "Ft Wagner" July 18th 1863.

| Co | Names | Rank | Co | Names | Rank |
|---|---|---|---|---|---|
| A. | 1 Andrew Benton | Sergeant | | | |
| | 2 Ralph Gardner | Corporal | G. | 67 Charles Body | Private |
| | 3 Henry Abbot | Private | " | 68 William H Meyers | " |
| | 4 James M. Allen | " | " | 69 Harrison Nichols | " |
| | 5 Henry F Burghardt | " | " | 70 Charles Stanbon | " |
| | 6 George W Duncan | " | " | 71 John Street | " |
| | 7 George F Ellis | " | " | 72 William Tyler | " |
| | 8 Joseph Ford | " | " | 73 William Underwood | " |
| | 9 Edward Hines | " | | | Sergeant |
| | ~~10 Sanford Jackson~~ | " | | | Corporal |
| | 10 Marshall Lamb | " | | | Private |
| | 12 Harrison Pierce | " | | | |

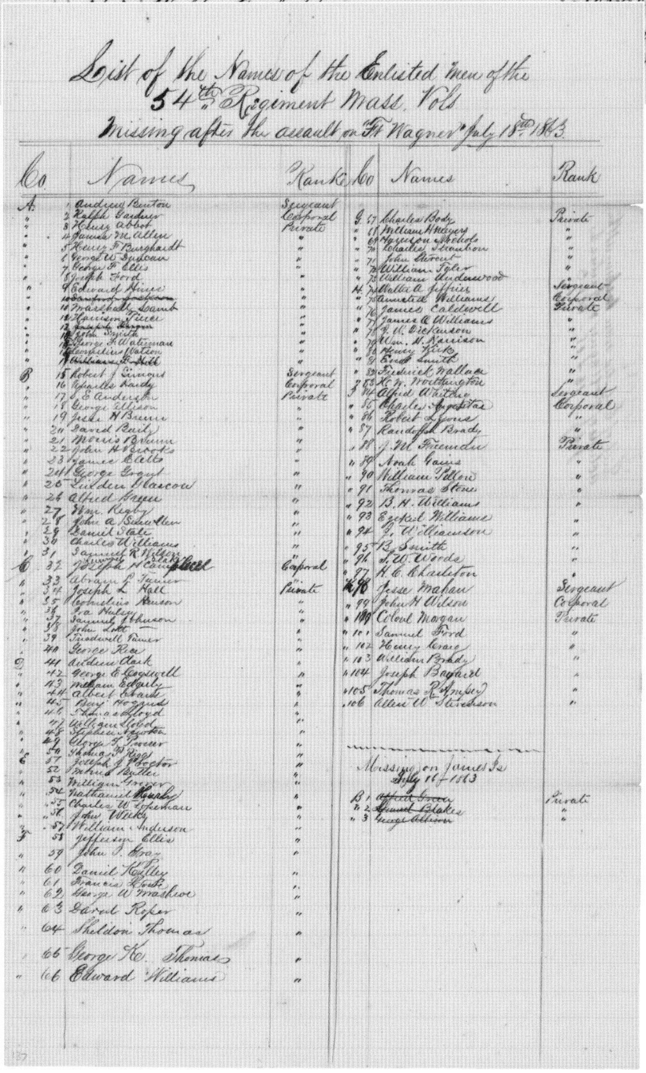

List of the Names of the Enlisted men of the
54th Regiment Mass. Vols
Missing after the assault on "Ft Wagner" July 18th 1863.

| Co | Names | Rank | Co | Names | Rank |
|---|---|---|---|---|---|
| A. | 1 Andrew Benton | Sergeant | | | |
| | 2 Ralph Gardner | Corporal | G. | 67 Charles Body | Private |
| | 3 Henry Abbot | Private | " | 68 William H Meyers | " |
| | 4 James M. Allen | " | " | 69 Harrison Nichols | " |
| | 5 Henry F Burghardt | " | " | 70 Charles Stanbon | " |
| | 6 George W Duncan | " | " | 71 John Street | " |
| | 7 George F Ellis | " | " | 72 William Tyler | " |
| | 8 Joseph Ford | " | " | 73 William Underwood | " |
| | 9 Edward Hines | " | H. | 74 Walter A. Jeffries | Sergeant |
| | ~~10 Sanford Jackson~~ | " | " | 75 Annistead Williams | Corporal |
| | 10 Marshall Lamb | " | " | 76 James Caldwell | Private |
| | 12 Harrison Pierce | " | " | 77 James A. Williams | " |
| | [illegible] | " | " | 78 J. H. Dickerson | " |
| | [illegible] Smith | " | " | 79 Wm. H. Harrison | " |
| | George Waterman | " | " | 80 Henry Hicks | " |
| | [illegible] | " | " | 81 [illegible] Smith | " |
| | [illegible] Hill | " | " | 82 Frederick Wallace | " |
| B. | 15 Robert J. Simmons | Sergeant | I. | 83 H. W. Worthington | " |
| | 16 Charles Hardy | Corporal | " | 84 Alfred Whiting | Sergeant |
| | 17 [illegible] | Private | " | 85 Charles [illegible] | Corporal |
| | 18 George Allison | " | " | 86 Robert Lyons | " |
| | 19 [illegible] H Bunn | " | " | 87 Randolph Brady | " |
| | 20 David Reid | " | " | 88 J. M. Friender | Private |
| | 21 Morris Brown | " | " | 89 Noah Gains | " |
| | 22 John H Brooks | " | " | 90 William Tillow | " |
| | 23 James Ellis | " | " | 91 Thomas Stone | " |
| | 24 George Grand | " | " | 92 B. H. Williams | " |
| | 25 Lisden Hascow | " | " | 93 Ezekiel Williams | " |
| | 26 Alfred Gayne | " | " | 94 G. Williamson | " |
| | 27 Wm. Kirby | " | " | 95 R. Smith | " |
| | 28 John A. Scantlen | " | " | 96 S. W. Woods | " |
| | 29 Daniel State | " | " | 97 H. C. Charleton | " |
| | 30 Charles Williams | " | K. | 98 Jesse Mahan | Sergeant |
| | 31 Samuel R. Wilson | " | " | 99 John H Wilson | Corporal |
| C. | 32 [illegible] | Corporal | " | 100 Colonel Morgan | Private |
| | 33 Abram P. Turner | Private | " | 101 Samuel Ford | " |
| | 34 Joseph L. Hall | " | " | 102 Henry Craig | " |
| | 35 Cornelius Hanson | " | " | 103 William Brady | " |
| | 36 Ira Wiley | " | " | 104 Joseph Bayard | " |
| | 37 Samuel Johnson | " | " | 105 Thomas R Amsey | " |
| | 38 John Lott | " | " | 106 Allen W Stevenson | " |
| | 39 Lindwell Turner | " | | | |
| | 40 George Rice | " | | Missing on James Is. July 16th 1863 | |
| D. | 41 Andrew Clark | " | B. | 1 Alfred Green | Private |
| | 42 George E Cogswell | " | " | 2 Samuel Blakes | " |
| | 43 William Edgely | " | " | 3 George Allison | " |
| | 44 Albert Hardy | " | | | |
| | 45 Ray Hogwood | " | | | |
| | 46 [illegible] Lloyd | " | | | |
| | 47 William Field | " | | | |
| | 48 Stephen Newton | " | | | |
| | 49 George T. Turner | " | | | |
| E. | 50 [illegible] Riggs | " | | | |
| | 51 Joseph J. Proctor | " | | | |
| | 52 [illegible] Miller | " | | | |
| | 53 William Grover | " | | | |
| | 54 Nathaniel Hurdle | " | | | |
| | 55 Charles W Lyman | " | | | |
| | 56 John Wilks | " | | | |
| | 57 William Anderson | " | | | |
| F. | 58 Jefferson Ellis | " | | | |
| | 59 John J. Gray | " | | | |
| | 60 Daniel H. Tilley | " | | | |
| | 61 Francis Houle | " | | | |
| | 62 George W Marlboro | " | | | |
| | 63 David Roper | " | | | |
| | 64 Sheldon Thomas | " | | | |
| | 66 George H. Thomas | " | | | |
| | 66 Edward Williams | " | | | |

opposite page:
**Letter from Col. E. Hallowell to Brigadier General Seymour describing fight at Fort Wagner, November 7, 1863**
*National Archives, Records of the Adjutant General's Office, 1780's–1917*

Col. E. N. Hallowell wrote this account of the battle of Fort Wagner almost four months after the attack. He highlighted the fall of the 54th Massachusetts Infantry Regiment's commanding officer, Col. Robert G. Shaw; the fight for the colors; and the loss of nearly half of the regiment. Colonel Hallowell is not a character in the film *Glory*.

above (detail) and right:
**"List of the Names of the Enlisted Men of the 54th Regiment Mass. Vols. Missing after the Assault on Ft. Wagner, July 18, 1863"**
*National Archives, Records of the Adjutant General's Office, 1780's–1917*

This list records all the enlisted men of the 54th Massachusetts Infantry Regiment missing—and presumed dead—after the assault on Fort Wagner. The total number missing was five sergeants, nine corporals, and eighty-six privates. It is the only document to appear in the film *Glory*, shown during the title sequence at the beginning of the DVD version.

## THE REEL D-DAY

D-day, the Allied invasion of Normandy, on the coast of France, on June 6, 1944, marked the beginning of the end of Nazi-occupied France during World War II. The cross-Channel offensive, which involved thousands of troops, ships, and aircraft that had assembled in the south of England, was the greatest amphibious attack the world had ever seen. The operation was an overwhelming success. By the end of D-day, some 156,000 Allied troops had breached the Nazis'"Atlantic Wall," which the leader of the Third Reich, Adolf Hitler, had thought impregnable.

Allied cameramen, who documented aerial and naval bombardments, parachute drops, and soldiers boarding transports and riding in landing craft, continued filming as the troops stormed ashore. Filmmakers have used that original footage, held by the National Archives, in documentaries and feature films. Original films and other firsthand visual records of D-day are as crucial to filmmakers as memos, reports, and photos are to historians. They contain a wealth of detail about what equipment was used, what the invasion beaches looked like, and even what the soldiers wore.

D-DAY DRESS PLATOON LEADER

Light Tan Towel

First-Aid Kit (MORE EASILY ACCESSABLE)

CANTEEN

COMBAT JACKET

Map-CASE, WATER-PROOF — Tied to Leg with thong

CARBINE

SHEATH KNIFE STRAPPED to BOOT

Boots "IMPREGNITED"

PARACHUTE-TYPE First-Aid Kit TAPED To SHEATH

HELMET with NET AN[D] CAMOUFLAGE — STRAP UP

Haversack, content[s] sealed in waterproof b[ag]

HAND GRENADE

BINOCULARS

LIFE-PRESERVE[R] ⅓ inflated, un[der] all other equip[ment]

2 carbine mag's

COMPASS

WIRECUTTERS (only handles show)

light leathe[r] gloves

ASSAULT-Typ[e] GAS-MASK

"JUMP" boots

inset:

**"D-Day Dress, Platoon Leader,"
by Lt. Jack Shea, 1944**
*National Archives, Records of the
Adjutant General's Office, 1917–*

The D-day assault was rigorous and required soldiers to be prepared for an attack that started at sea and ended on land. This drawing by combat historian Lt. Jack Shea, who was attached to the 29th Infantry Division, illustrates that soldiers were well equipped for an amphibious attack.

**"Landing on the coast of France under heavy Nazi machine gun fire …," by Chief Photographer's Mate Robert F. Sargent, June 6, 1944**
*National Archives, Records of the
U.S. Coast Guard (26-G-2343)*

In this D-day photograph, landing craft filled with assault troops are dropping their ramps on the Normandy coast. Coast Guardsmen manned the landing craft, which debarked troops near shore and immediately returned to the assault transports to pick up more. This dangerous shuttle continued throughout the day under enemy fire.

Page 6

# COAST FROM TRANSPORT AREA

Page 5

With maximum visibility, the coast should be seen from bridge height in the center of the Transport Area (20,000 yards off shore) from GRANDCAMP-LES-BAINS on the right to COUR-SEULLES on the left, with PORT-EN-BESSIN due south. The coast should appear to be practically level, with a maximum height to the right of PORT-EN-BESSIN, tapering slightly to the POINTE DU HOE on the right and to ARROMANCHES on the left. The 4 1/4 mile stretch of cliff from Exit D1 (VIERVILLE) to POINTE DU HOE should be distinguishable. The Exit valleys D1, D3, E1 and E3 are much less likely to show. On the left of the OMAHA Beach Area, to the left of FOX

GREEN Beach, the ten-mile stretch of cliff broken by valleys sho as ARROMANCHES. The only man-made objects which may be are the spires of VIERVILLE and COLLEVILLE, as well as the h MOULINS. PORT-EN-BESSIN and ARROMANCHES should be dis chances are against such visibility. At dawn the coast from ARR EN-BESSIN should be the most discernible section, being nearest

PORT-EN-BESSIN

655912 T67

NOT VISIBLE

HAMEL AU PRETRE

tween the beach and the bluff. Most of the houses visible in the assault area are on this flatland in Sector DOG. The houses are at Exit D1, at LES MOULINS (Exit D3), and in between, in two groups at HAMEL AU PRETRE.

# SECTOR DOG

# DOG GREEN
### 970 yards

The valley at Exit D1 marks the right flank of DOG GREEN Beach. The village of VIERVILLE will be visible above the bluff behind the right half of the beach. It has a church spire which should be conspicuous, if not already destroyed. Almost the entire beach is backed by a 6-12 foot seawall which slopes at an angle of 45 degrees. A number of breakwaters (retards) extends from the right portion of the wall. To the left, the wall diminishes in height and terminates 100 yards from the left flank of the beach, where a 4-8 foot wave-cut embankment begins. The left flank is marked by the central large house in the left group at HAMEL AU PRETRE. A paved road runs behind the wall and turns inland at Exit D1.

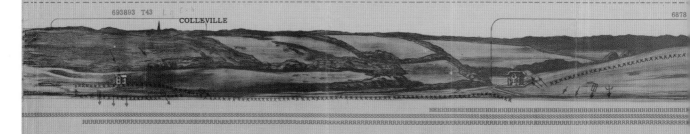

693893 T43       COLLEVILLE       6878

# SECTOR FOX

The right flank of FOX GREEN Beach is 300 yards to the right of the valley which carries Exit E3. This is 60 yards to the right of the point where Exit E3 cuts the beach. Exit E3 (which is a contin-uation of the shore road) bears inland just to the right of a stream which flows down the valley and fol-lows the stream's bank winding 300 yards to the left. It circles a lone white house at the base of the bluff and leads up the valley to COLLEVILLE. The left flank of the beach is at the point where the cliff rises from shore level and just to the left of where Exit F1 leaves the beach. This is the left

limit of the OMAHA Beach Area. The 200-foot bluff behind the beach is rough, woo It leads inland on the right to form the left side of the valley of Exit E3. There is o visible behind FOX GREEN Beach, which stands at the foot of the bluff slightly to th beach center. The white ruins of houses should be conspicuous between this house a church spire in COLLEVILLE may be visible above the bluff. The beach is backed bank 4-6 feet high for its entire length.

### D-day beaches "Coast from Transport Area" (Sector Dog Green and Fox Green), 1944
*National Archives, Records of the Allied Operational and Occupation Headquarters, World War II*

This map of Omaha Beach's Dog and Fox sectors was drawn from the perspective of the assaulting troops to help them recognize their landing areas and locate enemy positions. The mapmaker used information from low-level reconnaissance flights, agent reports, and special-operations troops who visited the beaches before the assault to ensure the map's accuracy.

## Film Holdings at the National Archives

The Federal Government has used motion pictures to document, inform, and persuade for almost as long as the medium has existed. Since its creation, the National Archives has recognized the historical value of film and has taken steps to ensure its accessibility and preservation for future generations. The National Archives holds audiovisual records created by Government agencies in the course of their work, as well as materials from private sources that relate to the history of the United States. Containing nearly 300,000 reels of film and more than 200,000 sound and video recordings, the audiovisual holdings of the National Archives are an invaluable resource for researchers.

# PRESIDENTS: CONFLICTS, CRISES, AND PEACE

Records in the National Archives document the multiple roles that U.S. Presidents serve, including head of state, commander-in-chief of the armed forces, and more. Photographers routinely expose the public face of the President—shaking hands with a foreign leader, visiting troops overseas, or waving from the door of Air Force One. But decisions such as ordering military action or planning a diplomatic mission are usually made outside the public eye after classified briefings and late-night meetings. As that information is declassified over time, it opens a window on Presidential decision making. Video and still photography capture public events as well as confidential conversations. Memoranda, speech drafts, and recordings and transcripts of restricted meetings reveal the candid thoughts and concerns of a President and his advisors.

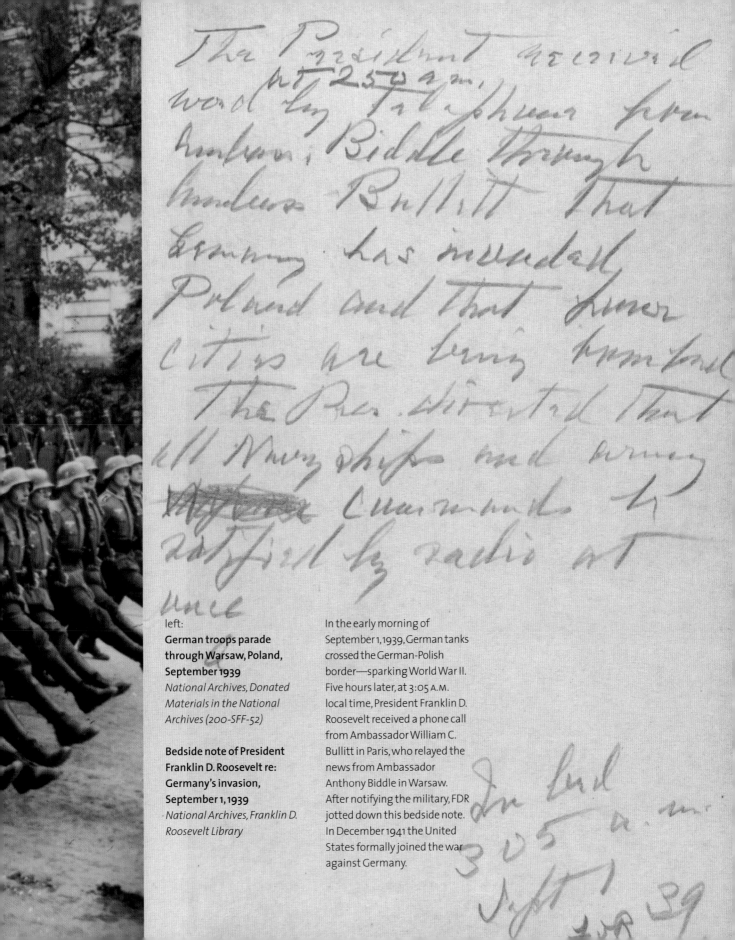

The President received word by telephone from Ambassador Biddle through Ambassador Bullitt that Germany has invaded Poland and that four cities are being bombed. The Pres. directed that all Navy ships and army commands be notified by radio at once

at 2:50 a.m.

In bed
3:05 a.m.
Sept 1 39
FDR

left:

**German troops parade through Warsaw, Poland, September 1939**
*National Archives, Donated Materials in the National Archives (200-SFF-52)*

**Bedside note of President Franklin D. Roosevelt re: Germany's invasion, September 1, 1939**
*National Archives, Franklin D. Roosevelt Library*

In the early morning of September 1, 1939, German tanks crossed the German-Polish border—sparking World War II. Five hours later, at 3:05 A.M. local time, President Franklin D. Roosevelt received a phone call from Ambassador William C. Bullitt in Paris, who relayed the news from Ambassador Anthony Biddle in Warsaw. After notifying the military, FDR jotted down this bedside note. In December 1941 the United States formally joined the war against Germany.

MRBM LAUNCH SITE 2
SAN CRISTOBAL
1 NOVEMBER 1962

MISSILE-READY TENT

FORMER LAUNCH POSITIONS

FORM

FOR

## Cuba, 1962

During the Cuban Missile Crisis of October 1962, the United States and the Soviet Union stood on the brink of nuclear war. The U.S. intelligence community had been closely monitoring a major arms buildup in Cuba: deliveries of Soviet weapons had recently increased to an alarming level. A U-2 spy plane had just photographed a site where the Soviet Union was preparing to install medium-range ballistic missiles, thereby putting the eastern United States at risk of a nuclear missile attack that could come on short notice. The threat was clearly imminent and severe.

While insisting that the Soviet Union remove its missiles from Cuba, President Kennedy worked feverishly to avert war. On October 22, Kennedy announced a naval blockade of Cuba. He demanded that the Soviet Union dismantle and remove their missiles. The Soviet Union tried to assure the United States that the buildup was defensive in nature, but Kennedy held firm, warning that "further action" might be needed if the buildup continued. Kennedy also declared a quarantine zone around Cuba, within which U.S. forces would intercept and inspect ships to determine whether they were carrying missiles.

**Aerial photograph showing medium-range ballistic-missile field launch site, San Cristobal No. 2, November 1, 1962**
*National Archives, John F. Kennedy Library*

opposite page:
**John F. Kennedy's notes from a meeting on the Cuban Missile Crisis, October 25, 1962**
*National Archives, John F. Kennedy Library*

During a Security Council meeting on October 25, the President scribbled several pages of notes. For a few tense days, Soviet vessels en route to Cuba avoided the quarantine zone while Chairman Khrushchev and President Kennedy communicated through diplomatic channels. On October 28, Khrushchev agreed to dismantle and remove the weapons and offered the United States on-site inspection in return for a guarantee that the United States would not invade Cuba.

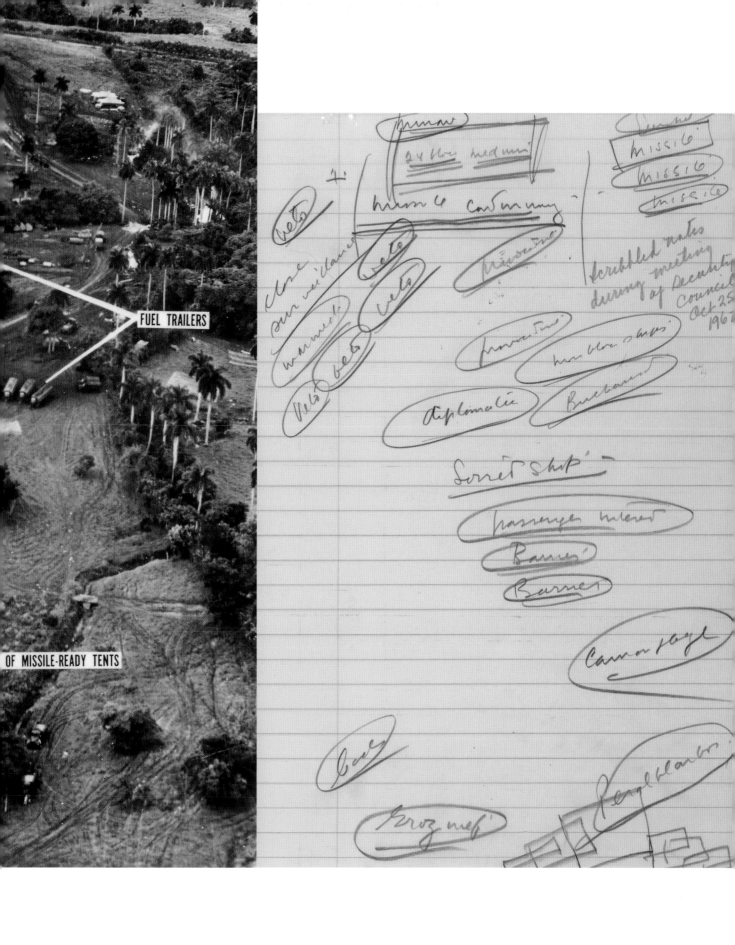

**President Richard M. Nixon and Chinese Premier Chou En-lai, Beijing, February 21, 1972**
*National Archives, Nixon Presidential Materials Project (C8487[24A])*

In February 1972 the formal visit of President Richard Nixon and Mrs. Nixon to Beijing to see Chinese Premier Chou En-lai launched improved relations between the United States and China after decades of Cold War hostilities.

below left:
**Anwar Sadat, Jimmy Carter, and Menachem Begin during one of the Camp David summit meetings, September 7, 1978**
*National Archives, Jimmy Carter Library (C-07284-21)*

opposite page:
**Draft of President George Bush's speech to the nation announcing military action against Iraq, January 15, 1991**
Page 1
*National Archives, George Bush Library*

opposite page (bottom):
**President Bush eating lunch with the troops, November 22, 1990**
*National Archives, George Bush Library (A-P17671[28])*

DRAFT #2
1/~~14~~/91
15

O----, ortin, At ~~this very minute~~ the allied ~~armed~~ air forces ~~are attacking~~ ~~countries~~ These attacks continue as I speak military targets in Iraq and Kuwait. Allied ground forces ~~have~~ are not ~~yet moved into Kuwait.~~ engaged.

The war started August 2nd when a brutal dictator invaded a small and helpless neighbor. Kuwait, a member of the Arab League and a nuke of the United Nations was crushed, Its people brutalized. Now the war has been joined.

This military action, taken in accord with the United Nations resolutions, follows months of seemingly endless diplomatic activity on the part of the United Nations, the United States and many, many other countries. Arab leaders sought what became known as an Arab solutin only to conclude that Saddam Hussein was unwilling to leave Kuwait. This past weekend, in a last ditch effort, the Secretary General of the United Nations went to the Middle East with peace in his heart. He came back from Baghdad with no progress at all in getting Saddam Hussein to leave Kuwait peacefully.

Now the 27 countries with for ... the Gulf area are prepared to see Saddam driven from Kuwai ... ... not fail. ~~and~~ and The legitimate security ... ... what is done secu ... As I report to you now, ai ... variety of targets in Ira ... Saddam Hussein's nuclear ... b ... chemical weapons facili ...

Each year, the National Archives declassifies hundreds of thousands of pages of documents. Top-secret records such as these may lose their classified status through a systematic review of records or one requested by an individual under an Executive order or the Freedom of Information Act. Declassified documents allow historians to better create a complete picture of the past. Throughout the declassification process, National Archives staff follows legal requirements designed to balance the public's right to know with the need for national security and the protection of intelligence sources.

## The Zimmermann Telegram

On January 16, 1917, in the midst of the European war that would later become known as World War I, German Foreign Minister Arthur Zimmermann sent this encoded message to the President of Mexico (it went first to Count von Bernstorff, a German diplomat in the United States, who transmitted it to the Mexican President in Mexico City). The telegram proposed a military alliance against the United States: in return for Mexican support in the war, Germany would help Mexico regain New Mexico, Texas, and Arizona from the United States.

British intelligence intercepted the telegram, deciphered it, and turned it over to the U.S. Government, which on March 1 revealed the contents to the American public. The United States had recently broken diplomatic relations with Germany in response to the German decision to begin unrestricted submarine warfare, which by the spring would take the lives of nearly 200 Americans. The Zimmermann Telegram further inflamed U.S. public opinion against Germany. Yet, so outlandish were its contents, many people doubted its authenticity.

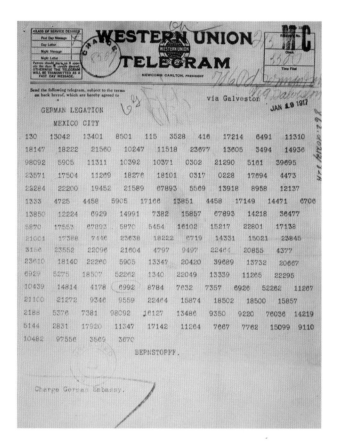

Zimmermann Telegram, as received by the German Ambassador to Mexico, January 19, 1917
*National Archives, General Records of the Department of State*

opposite page:
**Decode of the Zimmermann Telegram made by Edward Bell, March 2, 1917**
Page 4
*National Archives, General Records of the Department of State*

On March 2, 1917, the British asked Edward Bell, who worked in the American Embassy in London, to verify the secret message. Page four of Bell's decode mentions Texas, New Mexico, and Arizona. A photocopy of the telegram provided to the U.S. Department of State by Western Union validated the original telegram.

| | |
|---|---|
| 4458 | gemeinsam |
| 17149 | Friedenschluß . |
| | ⊙ |
| 14471 | |
| 6706 | reichlich |
| 13850 | finanziell |
| 12224 | unterstützung |
| 6929 | und |
| 14991 | Einverständnis |
| 7382 | unsererseits . |
| 158(5)7 | daß |
| 67893 | Mexico . |
| 14218 | in |
| 36477 | Texas |
| 5870 | ⊙ |
| 17553 | neu |
| 67893 | Mexico . |
| 5870 | ⊙ |
| 5454 | AR |
| 16102 | IZ |
| 15217 | ON |
| 22801 | A |

In the coded message below, every two letters represent a letter or number found in the grid. To decode the message, begin by grouping each set of two letters, starting with the first two letters (FG) and continuing through the message. (Some letter pairs will carry over from one line to the next.) The first letter is taken from the rows (horizontal axis) and the second from the columns (vertical axis). To decipher "FG," for example, find row "F" and column "G." Trace across the grid to their intersection at the letter "F." When you have completed identifying all the letter pairs, you've cracked the code. (The decoded message is given below.)

## Coded Message

FGAFA AAVXA DGAVX VADAD DVDDD VGA
VXVDX DVDDF AFDXG XGDDG AVFDV X
VAAFX GDADX VDDXD AVXXV
AAAVD AVXDA VVGDD XAVDG DXGXV XVDVF VVAFD XAVAF
VXDXV DFDAF XAVVV FAVAF VVVVV ADGXV AXAFD GGXFX AFAVV
ADGDF VFAXV DVXXF DAVXG DVAAF XGDAD XVDVF AVAFV FDGAV
AFVXV DAXAF DGXDA FAFVA AADGV VVVXV VDDFV VGDVD AVVXD
FVDVX DADXA F
AAAFA VDFVV VXVDA VFGFG XFDGV VGDDA DFFXV
XVDDF FDDX

## Grid

| | | Columns | | | | | |
|---|---|---|---|---|---|---|---|
| | | A | D | F | G | V | X |
| Rows | A | B | 2 | E | 5 | R | L |
| | D | I | 9 | N | A | 1 | C |
| | F | 3 | D | 4 | F | 6 | G |
| | G | 7 | H | 8 | J | 0 | K |
| | V | M | O | P | Q | S | T |
| | X | U | V | W | X | Y | Z |

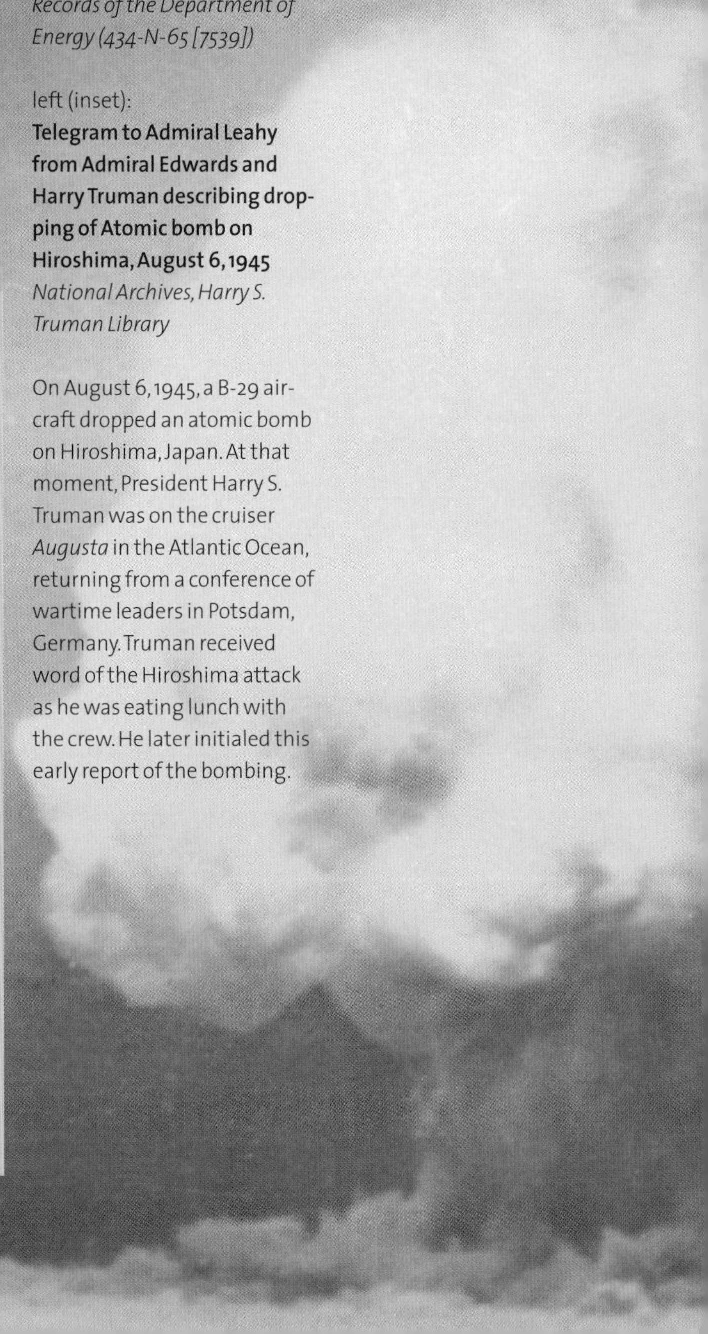

## The Atomic Bomb

On August 2, 1939, Nobel Prize–winning physicist Albert Einstein wrote to President Franklin D. Roosevelt about the possible military uses of atomic power and suggested that the Federal Government invest time and money into the creation of an atomic weapon. His letter is in the National Archives.

Eight months after the United States entered World War II, the Federal Government launched the Manhattan Project, an all-out but highly secret effort to build an atomic bomb—before the Germans did.

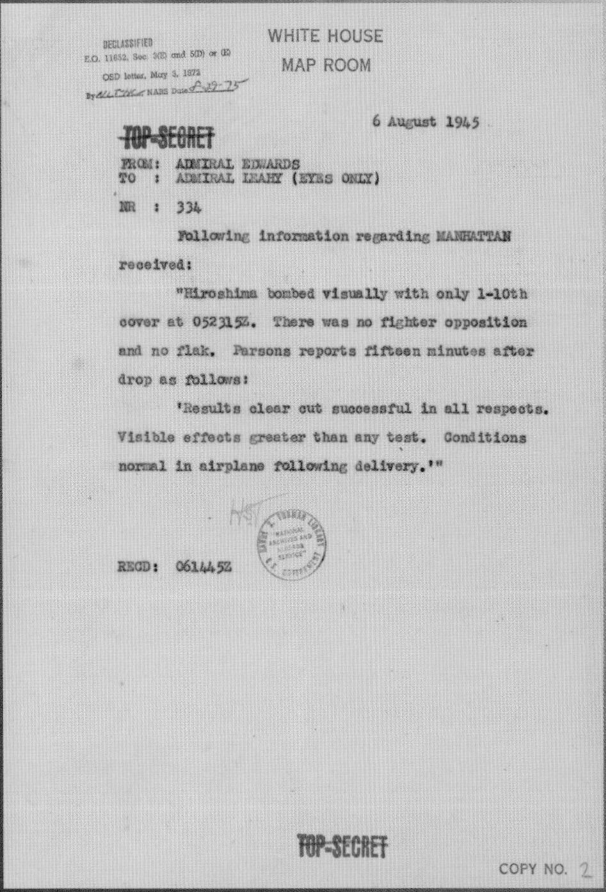

"Trinity" explosion at Los Alamos, Alamogordo, New Mexico, July 16, 1945
*National Archives, General Records of the Department of Energy (434-N-65 [7539])*

left (inset):
**Telegram to Admiral Leahy from Admiral Edwards and Harry Truman describing dropping of Atomic bomb on Hiroshima, August 6, 1945**
*National Archives, Harry S. Truman Library*

On August 6, 1945, a B-29 aircraft dropped an atomic bomb on Hiroshima, Japan. At that moment, President Harry S. Truman was on the cruiser *Augusta* in the Atlantic Ocean, returning from a conference of wartime leaders in Potsdam, Germany. Truman received word of the Hiroshima attack as he was eating lunch with the crew. He later initialed this early report of the bombing.

DECLASSIFIED
E.O. 11652, Sec. 3(E) and 5(D) or (E)
OSD letter, May 3, 1972
By _____ NARS Date 8-29-75

WHITE HOUSE
MAP ROOM

6 August 1945

~~TOP SECRET~~

FROM: ADMIRAL EDWARDS
TO  : ADMIRAL LEAHY (EYES ONLY)

NR : 334

Following information regarding MANHATTAN received:

"Hiroshima bombed visually with only 1-10th cover at 052315Z. There was no fighter opposition and no flak. Parsons reports fifteen minutes after drop as follows:

'Results clear cut successful in all respects. Visible effects greater than any test. Conditions normal in airplane following delivery.'"

RECD: 061445Z

TOP SECRET

COPY NO. 2

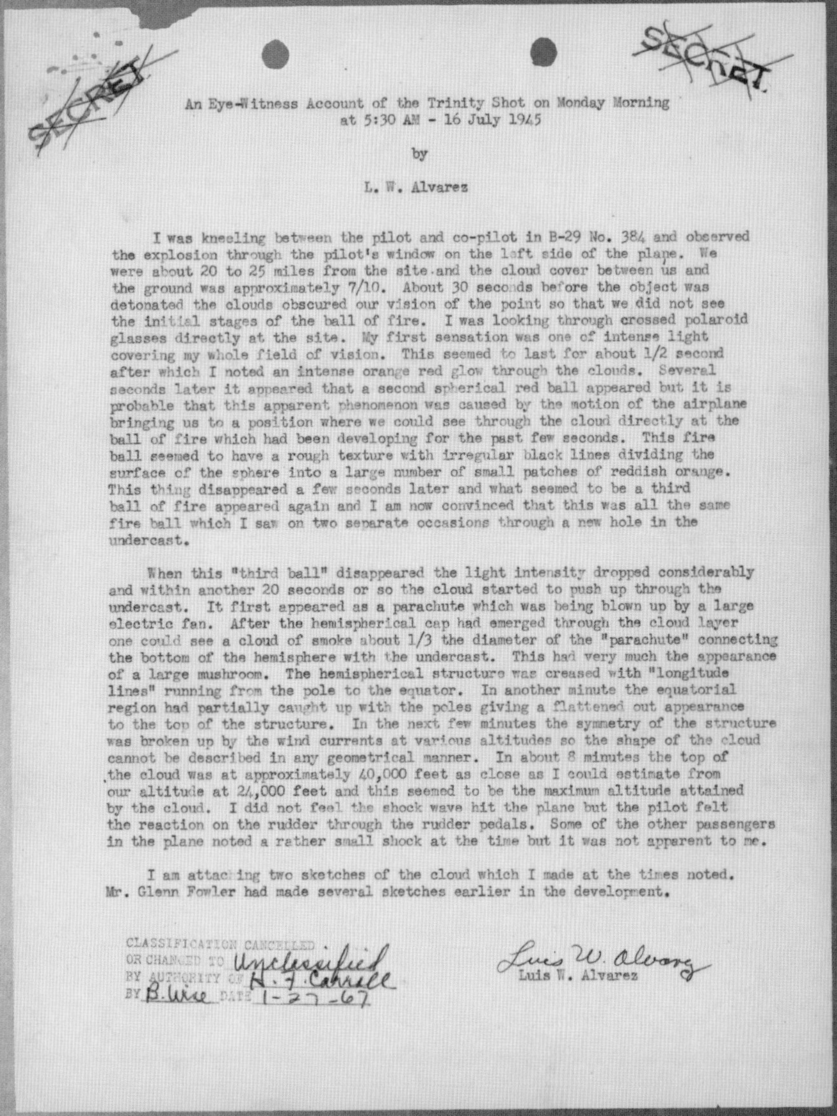

An Eye-Witness Account of the Trinity Shot on Monday Morning
at 5:30 AM - 16 July 1945

by

L. W. Alvarez

I was kneeling between the pilot and co-pilot in B-29 No. 384 and observed the explosion through the pilot's window on the left side of the plane. We were about 20 to 25 miles from the site and the cloud cover between us and the ground was approximately 7/10. About 30 seconds before the object was detonated the clouds obscured our vision of the point so that we did not see the initial stages of the ball of fire. I was looking through crossed polaroid glasses directly at the site. My first sensation was one of intense light covering my whole field of vision. This seemed to last for about 1/2 second after which I noted an intense orange red glow through the clouds. Several seconds later it appeared that a second spherical red ball appeared but it is probable that this apparent phenomenon was caused by the motion of the airplane bringing us to a position where we could see through the cloud directly at the ball of fire which had been developing for the past few seconds. This fire ball seemed to have a rough texture with irregular black lines dividing the surface of the sphere into a large number of small patches of reddish orange. This thing disappeared a few seconds later and what seemed to be a third ball of fire appeared again and I am now convinced that this was all the same fire ball which I saw on two separate occasions through a new hole in the undercast.

When this "third ball" disappeared the light intensity dropped considerably and within another 20 seconds or so the cloud started to push up through the undercast. It first appeared as a parachute which was being blown up by a large electric fan. After the hemispherical cap had emerged through the cloud layer one could see a cloud of smoke about 1/3 the diameter of the "parachute" connecting the bottom of the hemisphere with the undercast. This had very much the appearance of a large mushroom. The hemispherical structure was creased with "longitude lines" running from the pole to the equator. In another minute the equatorial region had partially caught up with the poles giving a flattened out appearance to the top of the structure. In the next few minutes the symmetry of the structure was broken up by the wind currents at various altitudes so the shape of the cloud cannot be described in any geometrical manner. In about 8 minutes the top of the cloud was at approximately 40,000 feet as close as I could estimate from our altitude at 24,000 feet and this seemed to be the maximum altitude attained by the cloud. I did not feel the shock wave hit the plane but the pilot felt the reaction on the rudder through the rudder pedals. Some of the other passengers in the plane noted a rather small shock at the time but it was not apparent to me.

I am attaching two sketches of the cloud which I made at the times noted. Mr. Glenn Fowler had made several sketches earlier in the development.

CLASSIFICATION CANCELLED.
OR CHANGED TO *Unclassified*
BY AUTHORITY OF *H. F. Carroll*
BY *B. Wise* DATE *1-27-67*

*Luis W. Alvarez*
Luis W. Alvarez

above (inset):

**"Eye-Witness Account of the Trinity Shot," by L. W. Alvarez, July 16, 1945**
*National Archives, Records of the Office of Scientific Research and Development*

The first test of the atomic bomb—which had been given the code name "Trinity" by the Manhattan Project's top scientist, J. Robert Oppenheimer—took place in the desert outside Alamogordo, New Mexico, on July 16, 1945. Manhattan Project physicist Luis Alvarez watched the explosion from a B-29 aircraft flying above the test site and recorded his account in words and drawings. In 1968, Alvarez won the Nobel Prize in physics.

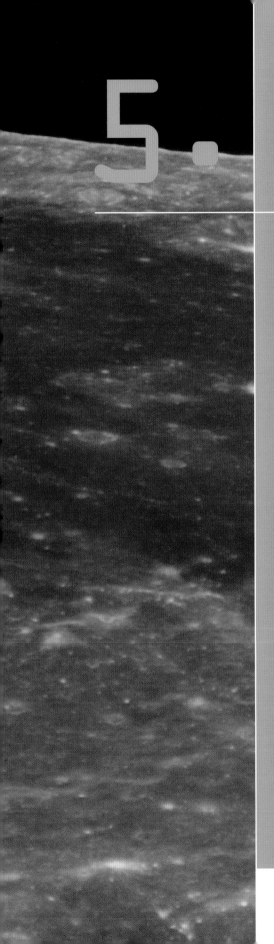

# 5.

# PROMOTE THE GENERAL WELFARE
## RECORDS OF FIRSTS AND FRONTIERS

Records illustrate the progress and challenges of our nation over time. Among the billions of records held at the National Archives are many that open a window on the human spirit and American ingenuity. Federal records are filled with documents and images of events that stand as milestones in the nation's life. Records often mark stages in the ever-changing definition of the Government's role in promoting the nation's general welfare —from the first photography of the West to contemporary satellite images, from the earliest patents to the first landing on the Moon.

The *Apollo 11* lunar module *(Eagle)* ascending to rendezvous with the *Apollo 11* command module *(Columbus)*, July 21, 1969
*National Archives, Records of the U.S. Information Agency (306-PSD-69-3099-C)*

ENTER>

The nation's collective memory of milestone events—such as the landing of *Apollo 11* on the Moon—is preserved in the records of the National Archives. Do you remember where you were that July day in 1969, when the first person walked on the Moon? Many Americans and people around the globe can recall exactly where they were and what they were doing when astronaut Neil Armstrong took "one giant leap for mankind."

In great detail, Federal records vividly chronicle activities across the nation and around the world on the days surrounding the first Moon landing. Among the records is a checklist of the procedures to be followed by the astronauts on their fifty-minute and two-hour walks on the lunar surface to take photographs, inspect equipment, and collect lunar soil. A page from President Richard Nixon's daily diary records an "interplanetary conversation" with astronauts Neil Armstrong and Edwin "Buzz" Aldrin at 11:45 P.M. on July 20. A telegram from the Minister of Foreign Affairs of Chile—one of many communications from foreign dignitaries sent to the U.S. Department of State—congratulates the United States on its "marvelous feat." The deck log from the USS *Hornet* for July 24, 1969, documents the ship's role in the recovery of the *Apollo 11* astronauts in the Pacific Ocean.

**"Daily Staff Journal" from the 101st Airborne Division, July 20, 1969**

*National Archives, Records of the U. S. Forces in Southeast Asia, 1950–1975*

Item 19 on an Army brigade's daily staff journal documents the exact time when Neil Armstrong walked on the Moon—11:03 A.M. The entry was made by a soldier in the 101st Airborne Division's 2nd Brigade stationed near Hue, Republic of Vietnam. Because Vietnam is on the other side of the International Date Line from the United States, the date is July 21, 1969 (instead of July 20).

| DAILY STAFF JOURNAL OR DUTY OFFICER'S LOG (AR 220-346) | | | | | PAGE NO. 3 | | NO. OF PAGES | |
|---|---|---|---|---|---|---|---|---|
| ORGANIZATION OR INSTALLATION | | LOCATION | | PERIOD COVERED | | | | |
| Hqs 2d Brigade 101st Abn Div | | Vic HUE, RVN YD638274 | | FROM HOUR 0001 | DATE 21 Jul 69 | TO HOUR 2400 | DATE 21 Jul 69 | |
| ITEM NO. | TIME IN / OUT | INCIDENTS, MESSAGES, ORDERS, ETC. | | | | ACTION TAKEN | | INI-TIALS |
| 17 | cont | 2 C 035920 W to 2 C 0292 S to 0290 E to present AO. | | | | | | |
| 18 | 1040 | (C) 2-501: At 1030 hrs 2-17 Cav wrking for Co D spotted 20 x NVA in bunkers vic YD55808. Request A/S ASAP. FAC on station at 1125 hrs. | | | | DO, DTOC, FAC | | GFE |
| 19 | 1110 | (C) 2-502: At 1103 hrs the first man walked on the moon. | | | | DO, DNCO | | JR |
| 20 | 1115 | (C) 2-501: At 1113 hrs Co D 3d Plat in contact YD579099. Pink Team on station. | | | | DO | | JR |
| 21 | 1230 | (C) 2-501: At 1220 hrs Cav Team in vic 558085 found 8 x bunkers and destroyed 2 x standing. Vic 579099 found 6 x bunkers and destroyed 3 x standing. Had 3" overhead cover. | | | | DO, S-2 | | JR |
| 22 | 1410 | (C) 2-501: Request EOD Team to report to Phung Dien to remove B-41 round from bunker and destroy it. Rocket was fired in attack 2 or 3 nights ago. | | | | DO, S-2 | | GFE |
| 23 | 1515 | (C) 2-501: At 1510 hrs 2d Plat Co B off PZ YD588358 and down on LZ Eagle Beach at 1526 hrs. | | | | DO, DTOC | | GFE |
| 24 | 1620 | (C) 2-502: At 1611 hrs Co B vic 039904 found large and 1 x small campfires, 1 x lot cut with machete and not over 1 week old. Estimated that a group of unknown size was | | | | 3 x DO, S-2 | | JR |
| TYPED NAME AND GRADE OF OFFICER OR OFFICIAL ON DUTY DAVID T. GIBSON, CPT, INF, S-3 AIR | | | | SIGNATURE | | DECLASSIFIED NND 873541 By SH/HcDen Date 8/22/00 | | |

DA FORM 1594 PREVIOUS EDITION OF THIS FORM IS OBSOLETE. PFC-Japan

CONFIDENTIAL

For more than two centuries, patents have protected the fascinating array of creations that have sprung from the minds of American authors and inventors. The Constitution authorizes Congress to grant inventors exclusive rights to their creations. Congress responded to this challenge in 1802 by establishing the Superintendent of Patents in the Department of State. The name and location of the office that the Superintendent oversees has changed over time, but the function has remained constant: the safeguarding of intellectual property.

The National Archives holds more than 2.8 million patent case files. The drawings that illustrate the inventions are often works of art in their own right, even if the inventions themselves may be difficult to recognize at first glance.

## WHAT AM I?

Look at these early patent drawings and guess what inventions they illustrate. (The answers are on the next page.)

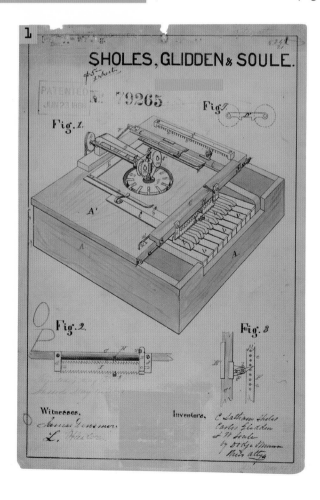

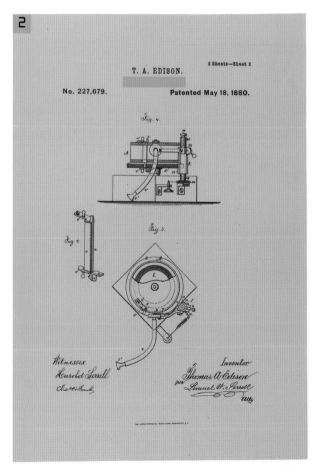

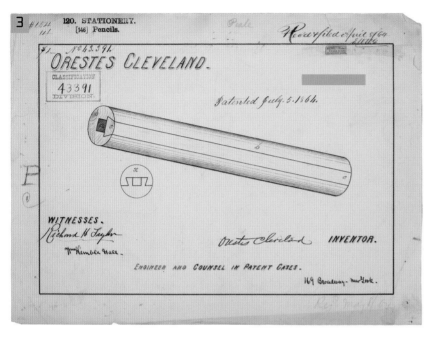

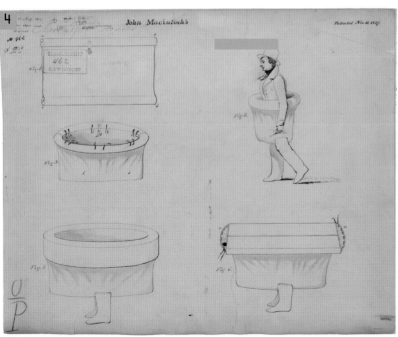

National Archives, Records of
the Patent and Trademark Office

4. Patent drawing for "Life
Boat," by John Macintosh,
November 11, 1837
National Archives, Records of
the Patent and Trademark Office

3. Patent drawing for a pencil,
July 5, 1864
National Archives, Records of
the Patent and Trademark Office

2. Patent drawing for
"Phonograph," by T. A. Edison,
May 18, 1880
National Archives, Records of
the Patent and Trademark Office

1. Patent drawing for
"Type-writer," by Sholes,
Glidden and Soule, June 23,
1868
National Archives, Records of
the Patent and Trademark Office

# FRONTIERS AND BOUNDARIES

Documents from America's past reveal how the United States expanded and the lines between states and other nations were drawn. At first, the thirteen British colonies were bounded by the Appalachians. But the frontier moved frequently, and as the country grew, new lands opened to large numbers of explorers and settlers. America's changing boundaries, both state and national, were created as much by diplomacy and political considerations as by the physical attributes of mountain ranges and riverbeds.

The National Archives holds many documents that describe the geography of America. In them, you can discover the land deals that physically shaped the nation and the vistas seen by early Western explorers, settlers, and surveyors of the West.

## Surveying the West

Photographs and other documents left by early Western survey parties enable us to see America's landscapes as they appeared in the 1800s. During the nineteenth century, the U.S. Government sent dozens of survey parties throughout the West to answer basic questions about newly acquired lands. Usually led by military officers or scientists, the parties crisscrossed the continent. They drew maps, filled journals with their observations, gathered natural and geological specimens, and covered canvasses and sketchbooks with rich detail. At mid-century, photographers joined the surveys. On large photographic plates, they recorded landscapes, Native Americans, and survey members at work.

"Grand Canyon, looking east from the foot of Toroweap," by John Hillers, ca. 1871
*National Archives, Records of the U.S. Geological Survey*
*(57-PS-431A)*

## The Struggle for the Pacific Northwest

Meriwether Lewis and William Clark staked out the American claim to the Pacific Northwest in 1804, but more than forty years later its borders were still not defined. The United States, Britain, Spain, and Russia all once claimed the vast Oregon territory, which stretched from the current northern border of California as far north as Alaska. The Convention of 1818 allowed U.S. and British citizens to occupy the territory without interference. Spain and Russia relinquished their claims by 1824.

Twenty years later, in the Presidential campaign of 1844, the territory was still in dispute. Democrat James K. Polk ran, and won, on a campaign to occupy the entire Oregon area, from the northern California boundary at latitude 54°40', the southern boundary of Russian Alaska. Although Polk's supporters used the slogan "Fifty-four Forty or Fight," the issue was settled peacefully in 1846, when the British accepted President Polk's offer to extend the Canadian boundary along the 49th parallel from the Rockies to the Pacific; the British, however, insisted on keeping the southern tip of Vancouver Island.

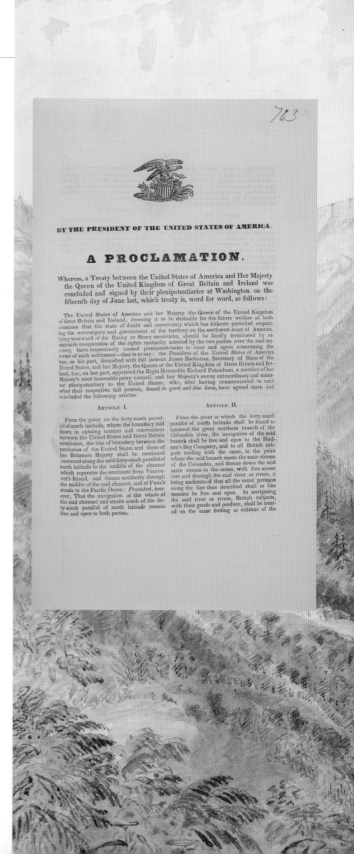

**"Camp Kishenehn (or Boundary Pass), Oregon Territory," by James W. Alden, ca. 1857**
*National Archives, Records of Boundary and Claims Commissions and Arbitrations*

inset:
**Proclamation by the President with the Queen of Great Britain and Ireland re: Oregon Territory, August 5, 1846**
*National Archives, Records of the Foreign Service Posts of the Department of State*

On August 5, 1846, President James K. Polk proclaimed the "Treaty with Great Britain, in Regard to Limits Westward of the Rocky Mountains." The treaty resolved the Oregon border dispute by drawing a straight line along the forty-ninth parallel. The line extended the existing boundary between the United States and Britain over the Rocky Mountains to the Pacific Ocean.

# CHANGING LANDSCAPES

Images from different periods that show America from above provide a striking look at how cities and landscapes have changed. Whether aerial or satellite, overhead imagery documents Earth's surface at a particular moment. It captures all visible features. No information is added or deleted. By comparing photos taken of the same place at different times, we can see towns grow or die, shorelines shift, lakes evaporate, and new buildings appear while old ones are demolished. The landscape seems to change before our very eyes.

1997

left (inset):
**Cape Canaveral, Florida,
February 14, 1943**
*National Archives, Records of
the Agricultural Stabilization
and Conservation Service (ON
30310, CYS-1C, exp. 9-10)*

main image:
**Kennedy Space Center,
July 31, 1997**
*National Archives, Records of
the Defense Intelligence Agency
(can 70011, exp. 18415-16)*

1943

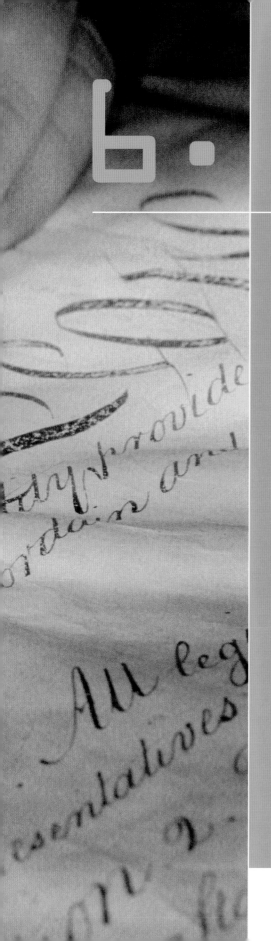

# 6. TO OURSELVES AND OUR POSTERITY
## ACCESS AND PRESERVATION

Every day, in every Federal agency, important documents are created. The President may sign an Executive order; the Congress may pass a bill; the Navy may gather data on a new fighter jet; new citizens may be naturalized. As the nation's record grows and changes, so does the National Archives. From rare parchments to electronic files, the National Archives preserves and makes available the records that tell America's story. As part of its mission to help citizens understand the importance of the records under its care, the National Archives is committed to preserving and making available those materials with equal access. With new technology come new challenges, which the National Archives is meeting head on to best preserve the historic record.

**A conservator examines the ink on page one of the official copy of the Constitution, letter by letter, using a binocular microscope and fiber-optic lighting.**

ENTER>

It's hard to put into words the excitement people feel when they see the Charters of Freedom—the Declaration of Independence, the Constitution, and the Bill of Rights. Yet until recently, the public has known little about how America's founding documents are preserved and displayed.

The Charters of Freedom were originally encased in the early 1950s by the National Bureau of Standards. All three documents were installed in what was then state-of-the-art technology—helium-filled, lead-sealed glass cases. But symptoms of glass deterioration, which could potentially obscure the public's view of the documents and damage the parchment, were discovered in the late 1980s.

To ensure the long-term preservation of these documents, National Archives staff assembled an interdisciplinary team of conservators, designers, engineers, and scientists, including staff from the National Institute of Standards and Technology (NIST), to design and build new cases that take advantage of the most up-to-date materials, technologies, and research. Conservators and the Exhibits staff at the Archives together with experts from other agencies worked to define the requirements for the seven encasements. They decided to fill the cases with inert argon gas, which would not react with the parchment and ink. As a safety measure, they would use sensors to monitor interior conditions within the encasement, checking for humidity and the presence of oxygen in the argon. Finally, for strength and stability, the team decided to make the frame out of titanium and the base out of an aluminum alloy.

NIST technical staff designed, improved, and tested several versions of the new encasement concept to establish that NARA's requirements could be met. The only remaining challenge was aesthetics. The titanium frame would be plated with an undercoat of nickel and finished with a layer of 24-karat gold to best complement the neoclassical architecture of the National Archives Rotunda. Having specified the materials and refined the design, the Archives authorized NIST to manufacture the final encasements. Next, conservators examined the documents, carefully looking at each pen stroke and letter under a microscope and using a gelatin adhesive to securely attach any lifting flakes of ink. They carefully humidified and flattened the delicate parchments, which had rippled over time.

Once conservation was complete, conservators placed the documents in their new cases, securing them with flexible plastic tabs that exert gentle pressure to keep the parchment smooth and in position. After five years of planning and conservation at a cost of almost $5 million, the newly encased Charters of Freedom were returned to the Rotunda for all to see.

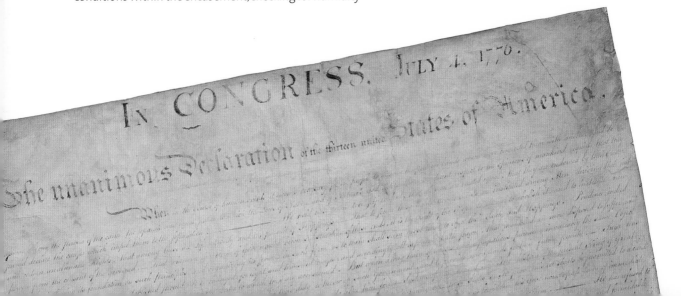

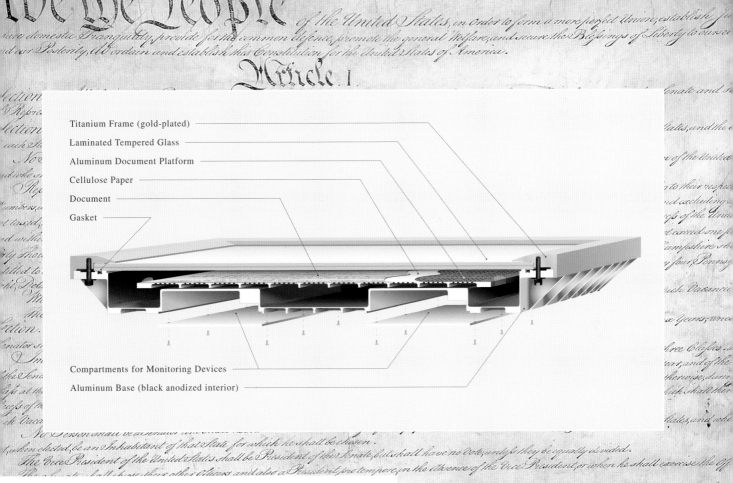

Titanium Frame (gold-plated)
Laminated Tempered Glass
Aluminum Document Platform
Cellulose Paper
Document
Gasket

Compartments for Monitoring Devices
Aluminum Base (black anodized interior)

oppostite page:

**Declaration of Independence, adopted July 4, 1776 (detail)**
*National Archives, General Records of the U.S. Government*

above:

**Constitution of the United States, adopted September 17, 1787 (detail)**
Page 1
*National Archives, General Records of the U.S. Government*

above (inset):

**Cross section of encasement**

New state-of-the-art encasements provide the best possible environment for the Charters of Freedom—America's founding documents. In February 2000 the transmittal page of the Constitution was sealed into a prototype encasement. After months of monitoring the document and the interior atmosphere, the design team finalized the case design.

right:

**Bill of Rights, ratified December 15, 1791 (detail)**
*National Archives, General Records of the U.S. Government*

Crumbling newspapers? Faded photos? Conservation experts at the National Archives spend a lot of time worrying about the health of documents.

Preserving records is one of the National Archives' most important missions. Archivists, technicians, conservators, and other specialists maintain the physical well-being of the nation's historic documents through environmental control and monitoring, appropriate storage techniques, and proper handling of records by researchers and staff.

When documents are already seriously damaged, conservators carry out surface cleaning, flattening, mending, and other treatments that improve the records' physical and chemical stability as well as their appearance.

Documents are subject to many kinds of damage. Light can fade ink or damage paper. Insects chew holes in documents. Liquids stain them. Heat and high relative humidity hasten deterioration. High humidity also promotes the growth of molds that weaken and stain paper.

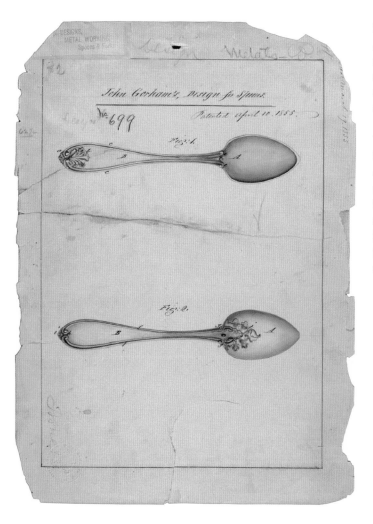

**Patent drawing for spoons, by John Gorham, 1855, before conservation treatment**
*National Archives, Records of the Patent and Trademark Office*

This 1855 patent drawing came to the National Archives with discoloration as well as deposits of dirt and grime on the paper. It also suffered large and small tears and some disintegration. Animal glue used in old repairs caused additional stains.

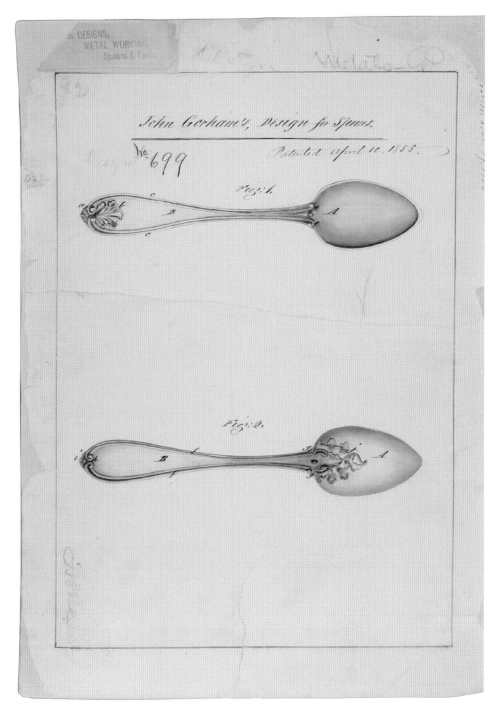

**Patent drawing for spoons, by John Gorham, 1855, after conservation treatment**
*National Archives, Records of the Patent and Trademark Office*

A National Archives conservator used a dry method to clean the paper surface and then bathed the drawing in purified water to remove water-soluable impurities. Handmade Japanese paper and wheat-starch paste were used to mend tears and fill areas of paper loss. The drawing was encapsulated in polyester film to protect it when it is handled.

## Where Should I Put My Favorite Photo of Grandpa?

Documents and photographs are extremely sensitive to light, high temperature, and high humidity. They are also at risk from other dangers. Proper storage, handling, and display can prevent damage to your family's treasures and reduce the chance that they will need extensive treatment in the future.

### WHERE DO YOU STORE YOUR FAMILY PHOTOS?

Explore this house to find the best place to safely store and display your family records. (See the next page for the recommendations by conservators at the National Archives.) For more information on preserving your family's documents, photos, and other treasures, visit *www.archives.gov/preservation/*.

### 1. In the attic?

Attics provide lots of room for storage but are subject to extreme temperatures and water leaks. The temperature should be comfortable for a human (65–70°F) and the relative humidity moderate (35–45%). Paper and photos are also attractive food sources and nesting material for insects and rodents.

### 2. In the basement?

Basements are usually cool, which is good for a document, but they are often damp and subject to flooding. They are also a popular home for insects.

### 3. On the den wall or fireplace mantel?

Choose an area away from sunlight and heat. This room is away from direct sunlight, but the fireplace exposes documents and photos to smoke and heat, which will damage them over time.

Regular frames are fine for everyday snapshots, but museum-quality matting and framing will help preserve important materials. To prevent light damage and fading, make display copies of important documents, and store the originals in a good storage container.

### 4. Under the coffee table?

Organizing photos in an album makes good sense. Look for albums made with acid-free paper or a stable plastic such as polyester. Avoid self-stick albums and tapes for any photo or document you intend to keep for a long time. Also avoid plastic pocket albums made from polyvinyl chloride.

### 5. In a file cabinet?

This is a good choice for home storage. Folders made of acid-free paper provide additional protection. Storage boxes that meet preservation requirements are a good alternative. A metal file cabinet is preferable to a wood cabinet.

### 6. On the home computer?

Digitization offers easy access to photos and documents. Once images are scanned, you can view them electronically and make hard copies without damaging the originals. But keep your originals. Today's electronic storage medium will become obsolete or deteriorate long before your important paper documents or photographs do. It is important to make back-up copies and to transfer data to newer versions of software as technology changes.

## THE DIGITAL CHALLENGE

As more Government records are created in a variety of electronic formats, National Archives staff searches for new ways to preserve and provide access to digital records. In 2025, will you be able to retrieve a Presidential e-mail sent today with the same ease by which you can read a Civil War telegram? How will you know it's authentic? Will veterans serving in the military today be able to access copies of their service records? Will a filmmaker creating a documentary be able to view digital photographs taken in 2003?

To meet its mission, the National Archives must find answers to these and many other challenging questions. In recent years, National Archives staff has been working with others inside and outside Government to devise ways to manage and preserve electronic records and to make them accessible—to anyone, anywhere, any time.

**At the National Archives, the shelves are emptying of canisters for computer tapes as data is migrated from tape reels to hard drives.**

NARA? The acronym stands for National Archives and Records Administration. Located across the United States, NARA's Presidential libraries and regional archives, as well as the National Personnel Records Center in St. Louis, Missouri, offer visitors a wealth of resources for study and an abundance of educational programs. Records in Presidential libraries chronicle the major events of a Presidency and also offer glimpses into the personal lives of those who have occupied the White House. Regional records focus on Federal activities that were undertaken by agency field offices. They often have a distinctive local flavor.

below (detail) and overleaf:
**This map of the United States is made up of 3,750 records from the National Archives. Photomosaic® by Robert Silvers, *www.photomosaic.com*. All rights reserved.**

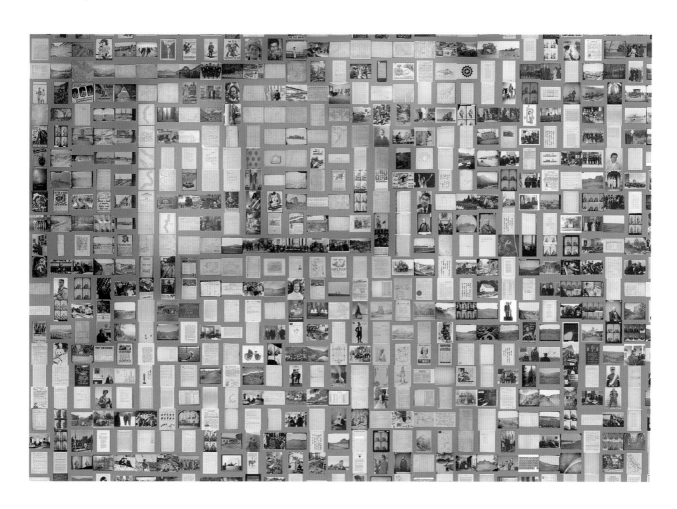

TO OURSELVES AND OUR POSTERITY

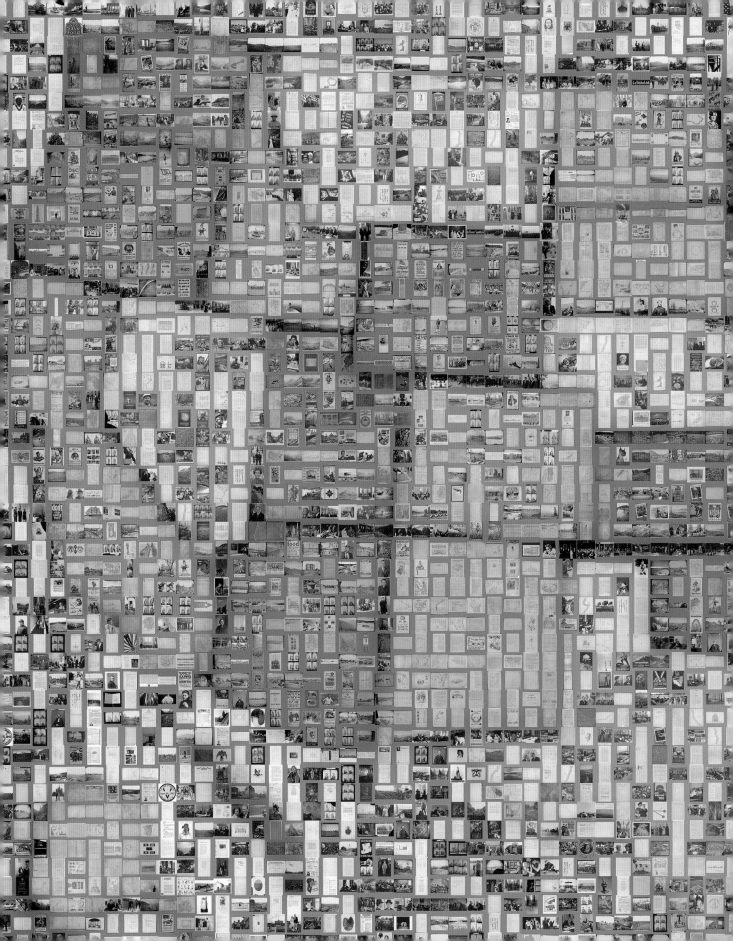

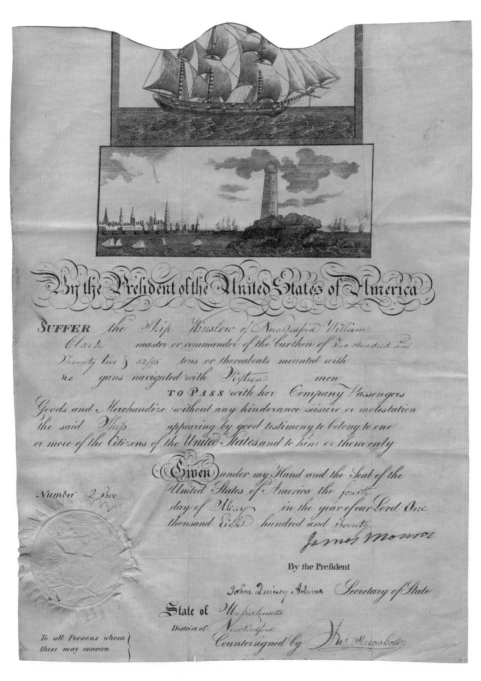

**A Mediterranean passport for the ship *Winslow*, signed by President James Monroe, May 4, 1820**

*National Archives–Northeast Region (Boston), Records of the U.S. Customs Services*

This 1820 passport signed by President James Monroe and Secretary of State John Quincy Adams allowed ships owned by the United States to sail the Mediterranean Sea without fear of interference by pirates.

Presidential campaign poster for Herbert Hoover and running mate Charles Curtis, 1928
*National Archives, Herbert Hoover Library (71-18-42)*

This Herbert Hoover campaign poster from 1928 was published by the Republican State Central Committee, Des Moines, Iowa.

bottom right:
**Faneuil Hall and Quincy Markets, Boston, Massachusetts, 1939**
*National Archives–Northeast Region (Boston), Records of the Works Progress Administration*

This print of Faneuil Hall in Boston was created by an artist working for the Works Progress Administration's Federal Art Project.

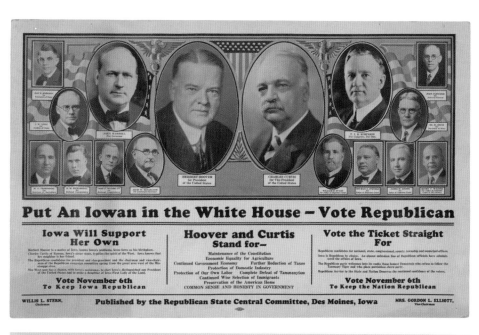

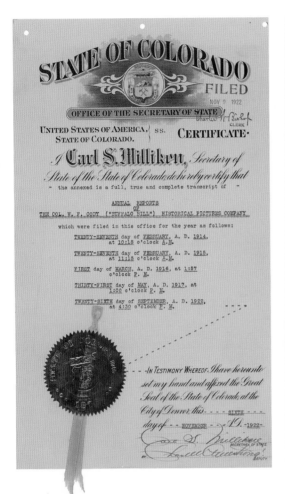

**Cover of Tongass National Forest map, 1963**
*National Archives–Pacific Alaska Region (Anchorage), Records of Temporary Committees, Commissions, and Boards*

This Forest Service map of the Tongass National Forest in Alaska is among the records of the Federal Field Committee for Development Planning in Alaska.

**Page from annual report of the Col. W. F. Cody "Buffalo Bill" Historical Pictures Company, November 6, 1922**
*National Archives–Rocky Mountain Region (Denver), Records of the District Courts of the United States*

The Annual Reports of the Col. W. F. Cody ("Buffalo Bill") Historical Pictures Company were exhibits in a District Court case between the company and the Colonial Amusement Company et al., September 8, 1913, to October 19, 1922. The case centered on copyright infringement involving the improper use of Cody's image and name, "Buffalo Bill."